An Introduction to Spiritual Direction

D1563962

An Introduction to Spiritual Direction

A Psychological Approach for Directors and Directees

Chester P. Michael

PAULIST PRESS
New York/Mahwah, N.J.

BV
5053
.M53
2004

Scripture extracts are taken from the New Revised Standard Version, Copyright © 1989, by the Division of Christian Education of the National Council of the Churches of Christ in the United States of America and reprinted by permission. Excerpt from *The Autobiography of St. Thérèse of Lisieux: The Story of a Soul,* copyright © 1957 by Doubleday, a division of Random House, Inc. Used with permission.

Book design by Lynn Else
Cover design by Bright i Design

Copyright © 2004 by Chester P. Michael

All rights reserved. No part of this book may be reproduced or transmitted in any form or by any means, electronic or mechanical, including photocopying, recording, or by any information storage and retrieval system without permission in writing from the Publisher.

Library of Congress Cataloging-in-Publication Data

Michael, Chester P.
    An introduction to spiritual direction : a psychological approach for directors and directees / Chester P. Michael
        p.   cm.
    Includes bibliographical references.
    ISBN 0-8091-4174-4 (alk. paper)
    1. Spiritual direction. I. Title.

BV5053 .M53 2004
253.5'3—dc22

                                                        2003019580

Published by Paulist Press
997 Macarthur Boulevard
Mahwah, New Jersey 07430

www.paulistpress.com

Printed and bound in the
United States of America

Contents

Preface

Religious education is a life-long task. We must never think of religious education as applicable only to children and teenagers. If anything, if adults are to grow spiritually, they must seek knowledge to attain understanding and wisdom to strengthen and live their faith. Religious education should extend throughout our lifetime. Religion is a subject that only adults can fully comprehend. This is especially true of the Christian religion. It involves the study of religious mysteries that have been revealed to us by Jesus Christ, by the biblical writers, and by countless other wisdom figures.

Of all the forms of religious education, individual spiritual direction can perhaps be the most important. Individual spiritual direction takes into account the uniqueness of each human being and adjusts the teaching to fit the needs of that person. This requires wisdom and knowledge on the part of the spiritual director.

The contents of this book are addressed primarily for the benefit of spiritual directors. However, almost everything found in this book will be helpful also for the person seeking direction to understand the process and breadth of the undertaking.

In no way does this book say all that needs to be said in order to train a person to be a good spiritual director. However, this book does give the basic knowledge needed by anyone who wishes to be a director. Spiritual direction is an art that must be studied and practiced for many years in order to reach proficiency. However, the need for spiritual direction today is so great that anyone with a modicum of knowledge can be an effective director.

John Yungblut and some other authors object to the use of the term *spiritual direction*. They prefer *spiritual guidance*. However, *direction* is the traditional term that has been used for many centuries, so I prefer to keep this term. I understand Yungblut's preference for *guidance* and I like the title of his book, *The Gentle Art of Spiritual Guidance*. The director must be careful not to impose his or her will on the directee. Spiritual direction is given primarily by way of suggestion and so is indeed a gentle art. However, there are times when the director needs to confront the directee in a gentle, loving way.

This book contains approximately one-third of the material covered in a two-year training course for spiritual directors. Altogether some fifty tools for spiritual direction are given during the two years of a Spiritual Direction Institute. The tools given in this book are the basic ones needed in spiritual direction. Implemental tools will be contained in another volume.

A substantial part of this two-year training program in the Spiritual Direction Institute is based on the depth psychology of Carl Jung. Along with many others I see great value of Jungian psychology for spiritual direction. Only a small portion of this book concerns Jungian psychology, primarily, chapter 11, the Four Steps of Individuation. However, chapter 13 touches on the value of a knowledge of temperament and psychological type in spiritual direction. The book *Prayer and Temperament*, by Michael and Norrisey, is recommended to all spiritual directors and directees.

Other valuable aids to both spiritual direction and individual spiritual growth would be knowledge of the spirituality of the Enneagram and spiritual journaling. Books on these two topics are numerous. We have suggested a few in the bibliography.

CHAPTER 1

History of Spiritual Direction

The present popularity of spiritual direction is part of the whole search for inner meaning and personal fulfillment that our present age finds so attractive. It would seem that along with so many other new discoveries, present-day humankind has come to a deeper realization of the need and value of developing each person's personality to a higher degree of wholeness. Actually, the only thing new about this is the widespread interest in this topic of self-development. The history of spiritual direction is as old as the known history of the human race. Among the Israelites of the Old Testament, we find Moses giving spiritual direction to the people in the desert and appointing seventy-two elders to assist him in this task of spiritual direction. We find the priest Eli directing the boy Samuel how to answer the Lord when God called. The prophet Nathan directed David concerning the building of a Temple to the Lord. One of the most dramatic instances of spiritual direction in the Bible is found in the twelfth chapter of the Second Book of Samuel. Nathan rebukes King David for the double sin of adultery and murder. Other examples would be Elijah directing Elisha, and Sirach directing those under him. Four of the five books of the Pentateuch are mostly books of spiritual direction for the Israelite people.

During New Testament times Jesus spent the greater portion of his public ministry giving spiritual direction to his disciples.

Rabbi Gamaliel directed the young Jewish rabbis under him, among whom was Saul of Tarsus. The whole body of Pauline Epistles may be seen as spiritual direction on the part of Paul for his converts. Later, the desert Fathers of the fourth and fifth centuries continued the tradition of spiritual direction for the neophytes who flocked to the desert to gain wisdom from the teachings of these anchorites. Similarly, St. Augustine in North Africa at this same time was directing the monasteries of religious men and women under his charge and writing a rule of life for them to follow in their growth toward holiness. In the succeeding centuries the Benedictine abbots in the West, the monks of Mt. Athos in Greece, and the Starets in Russia, are all a part of the tradition of spiritual direction during the first Christian millennium.

This tradition of spiritual direction continued throughout the second Christian millennium in the Benedictine, Cistercian, and other monasteries of men and women, among the Mendicant Orders of the Franciscans, Dominicans, and other religious orders. In the fourteenth century, the *Devotio Moderna* movement in the Low Countries of Holland and Belgium extended this practice of spiritual direction to lay men and women. Similarly, most of the religious orders established Third Orders and Oblate groups among the laity for the primary purpose of furnishing spiritual direction to women and men in the world. In the sixteenth century, the Carmelites and Jesuits extended the practice of spiritual direction not only among their own fellow religious but also among the ordinary lay women and men of the world.

In the seventeenth century, St. Francis de Sales and St. Vincent de Paul in France and St. Philip Neri in Rome made the custom of spiritual direction for lay men and women even more popular. The tradition continued in a very special way in France throughout the eighteenth and nineteenth centuries. At the end of the nineteenth century, two well-known French priests and an English layman made the practice of spiritual direction for the laity especially popular. The two priests are Abbe Huvelin and Abbe Saudreau. Huvelin was the spiritual director for Baron von Huegel, the English layman whose letters to his niece Gwendyln are some of the best writings we have on spiritual direction. Carl Jung once stated that the person in all history who came closest to his own methods of healing souls was that of Abbe Huvelin in France in the nineteenth century.

Carl Jung and his disciples have given a scientific basis to the practice of spiritual guidance. Sociologists and historians have also discovered a similar tradition of spiritual guidance in other cultures besides Judaism and Christianity. These would be the Eastern Guru among the Hindus and Buddhists, the shamans of the more primitive cultures of Africa and among the Eskimos, and the Medicine Man of the American Indians. The discovery of the unconscious by depth psychologists and its powerful influence on our conscious activities has added a whole new dimension to the importance of spiritual guidance. German psychologist Father Josef Goldbrunner has beautifully expressed this connection between psychology and spirituality by the title of one of his books, *Holiness Is Wholeness*. Grace and nature are not in opposition to one another but form a team to aid each of us on our life's journey toward the maturity for which God has destined us. Therefore, any spiritual director today who would neglect to make full use of the findings of depth psychology in guiding persons toward holiness would be neglecting a very important aid in this whole process of spiritual growth.

In early Oriental Christianity spiritual direction seems to have begun primarily with the formation of the monks in the desert communities of Egypt, Palestine, and Syria. The spiritual director was given the title of abba or father. St. Anthony of

Egypt would be one such example. Abba Isaac is the one to whom John Cassian especially refers when writing of the spiritual direction given in the Egyptian desert. In the western part of the Roman Empire, John Cassian, St. Cyprian, St. Ambrose, St. Jerome, St. Augustine, and St. Benedict are some of the more famous directors. During the dark ages spiritual direction was confined for the most part to monks and nuns in monasteries and convents. The Irish monks who evangelized northern Europe in the eighth and ninth centuries introduced spiritual direction to the laity of France and the Germanic countries. The seventeenth century has been called the Golden Age of spiritual direction. In the twentieth century the discovery of depth psychology has added greatly to the value of spiritual counseling. Once again we seem to be on the verge of a new golden age of spiritual direction. Witness the profusion of books on the subject that are being published at the present time.

CHAPTER 2

What and Why of Spiritual Direction

Spiritual direction is usually a one-to-one relationship with another individual for the purpose of obtaining spiritual guidance. By obtaining the help of an interested and wise human being, we are assisted on our journey of faith toward the kingdom of God. A spiritual director or soul friend will encourage, guide, advise, confront, and challenge us on the path toward holiness. The goal of spiritual direction is to help us fulfill our God-given destiny on Earth, to carry out the purpose of our existence, to fulfill all the duties of our state in life, to save our souls after death in heaven, and to become saints. We meet with a spiritual director or friend at regular intervals of time—monthly, bimonthly, quarterly—to give an account of our stewardship in God's service. This accountability then becomes an added grace and help in our spiritual life.

One meets regularly with the spiritual director for approximately an hour. At that time one reports on the successes and failures in the areas of prayer, charity, ministry, self-discipline, even bodily care. Problems, faults, questions, difficulties that have arisen will be discussed, as will struggles, temptations, and failures with a view to finding a proper solution to them. Relationships with God, other individuals, the community-at-large, and oneself will be explored. Special moments of grace or faith experiences in our relationship with God will be shared.

Dreams might be shared and an effort made to understand what one's unconscious is trying to reveal. Any spiritual reading, especially reading of the Bible, that one has done since the last meeting is reported and discussed.

It is recommended that the director and directee pray together for discernment and help of the Holy Spirit. Then a resolution regarding future progress in prayer, ministry, self-discipline, and care of the environment is agreed on and perhaps written down to make sure it is clearly understood. It is advisable that two copies of this Personal Growth Plan be made, one for the directee and one for the director. In this way accountability at the next spiritual direction session can be assured. Care should be taken not to prolong the session much beyond an hour unless some very special problem is involved. In this way the actual purpose of the meeting is accomplished without a waste of time in small talk.

Spiritual direction will be concerned with the four basic relationships of love with which our life on Earth is involved. They are love of God, love of others, a proper love of ourselves, and a love of nature. The love of God is expressed primarily in a regular, daily regime of prayer. As far as possible an effort is made to center one's whole life in God and the doing of God's Will. For this to be successful, one will strive to attain a good, positive image of God as all-good, all-wise, all-loving, all-powerful, always faithful to his word and promises. Every spiritual direction session will address this relationship of love for God.

The relationship of love of neighbor is absolutely essential for any true follower of Jesus Christ. Jesus insists, "By this everyone will know that you are my disciples, if you have love for one another" (John 13:35). Jesus also gave his disciples a new commandment of love of neighbor that goes far beyond the Mosaic command to love your neighbor as you love yourself. Jesus says, "I give you a new commandment, that you love one another. Just as I have loved you, you also should love one another" (John 13:34). This love of others may be divided into the loving care of other individuals and the loving service we give to the groups or communities to which we belong. Such groups would be our families; our work group; local, state, and national communities; the Church, local, national, and international; the whole human race, past, present, and future. In each spiritual direction session these different relationships with others are considered and suitable decisions are made for successfully and lovingly fulfilling them. All of these relationships of love of neighbor can be lumped under the title of *ministry*.

A proper love of one's self may conveniently be divided into our relationship with our inner self—our spiritual being, psyche, or soul—and our relationship with our body. We have the responsibility to take the proper care of both body and soul since each of them is God's gift to us to enable us to carry out the purpose of our existence on Earth. We care for our inner self by developing and using all those human faculties that God has endowed our nature: mind, will, memory, feeling, senses, imagination, intuition, instinct, and so on. We care for our bodies by using reasonable care to maintain good bodily health. Each meeting with a spiritual director will address one's inner, spiritual growth as well as bodily care.

A fourth area of love concerns our relationship with nature and the environment. God calls us to be good stewards of all the natural resources of the Earth. There is a sufficiency of resources for the whole human race provided a proper distribution is made of the goods of God's creation.

When we consider these four areas of concern, no one will be at a loss to know what to discuss with a spiritual director. In fact, so much is involved that many sessions may be required to cover all the concerns of one's life and growth. Ordinarily, a director will not agree to give ongoing direction to a person who is without real seriousness of purpose about growth in the four relationships of love of God, neighbor, self, and nature. Without this seriousness of purpose, the effort given to this task of spiritual direction will be a waste of time for both director and directee.

It is recommended that some time be given to mutual prayer either at the beginning or end of each session. The director may read aloud an appropriate passage from scripture. The director may lay hands on the head of the directee and pray for God's blessing and the Holy Spirit upon the directee.

By seeking spiritual direction from a trusted friend, counselor, or director, one attempts to obtain a more objective view of one's life and its progress in spirituality. The spiritual director is there to suggest, encourage, guide, and warn of dangers and roadblocks on the path of holiness. Spiritual direction is never a case of blind obedience to another human being. It is simply an openness to the insights and suggestions of a third party who is trustworthy and has good experience and wisdom regarding the four relationships of love. God commands us to love God, neighbor, self, and nature. Anyone who helps us fulfill these commands of love is acting as our spiritual director.

The directee will be encouraged to go in whatever direction is of the greatest interest or felt need. The task of the spiritual director is to make sure that all the bases are covered sooner or later. Both director and directee will keep themselves constantly open to the guidance of the Holy Spirit in determining the particular direction God wishes. With such an attitude, it is inevitable that some blind alleys or cul-de-sacs will be encountered. When this becomes apparent, humility is needed by both director and directee to admit the mistake, return to space one, and begin a new probing of God's Will for the directee. As long as we keep trying to discern and do God's Will, God is satisfied and our spiritual journey of faith is a success.

Ordinarily we think of spiritual direction as a one-on-one experience. However, spiritual direction may also be given in a group setting. Together a group may seek to discern God's Will not only for group activities but also for decisions for the guidance of individuals. Guided and directed retreats offer a great deal of spiritual direction for the individuals who attend such retreats. Enough spiritual direction may be given during an extended directed retreat to take care of the normal needs for direction for the next twelve months, unless special problems arise.

Why Spiritual Direction

There is a tremendous hunger and thirst today for spiritual guidance and help on one's journey of faith toward the kingdom of God. We live in very confused, uncertain, changing times. Many of our old standards of value have become discredited. The worldly goals we have been pursuing no longer satisfy or fulfill our needs. People are confused, frustrated, disappointed, afraid, and insecure. Our whole future is uncertain. Realizing that there is something seriously lacking in their lives, many people today stumble almost unknowingly into the pursuit of holiness. Finding themselves now on this new, strange road of spirituality, they look desperately for help and guidance to know what they should do with this new interest in their life. More and more people today are experiencing a hunger for the wholeness and fulfillment that worldly goals are unable to fulfill. They find themselves arriving at the same conclusion that St. Augustine did sixteen hundred years ago that our hearts are made for God and won't rest until they rest in God.

Our educational system, both public and religious, has been woefully lacking in giving people proper moral and spiritual guidance. People today are highly educated in worldly topics but miserably ignorant of spiritual and religious matters. Even some of those who have attended parochial schools and religious colleges are basically uneducated in the area of spirituality. Most Catholics and other Christians stopped attending religious classes after confirmation and before reaching adulthood. Yet the Christian religion and spirituality are topics that only an adult is able fully to comprehend. Children and adolescents are able to attain a knowledge of many religious facts but religious education is primarily a task for mature adults. Only recently have the Christian churches begun to take seriously this task of adult religious education. Countless adult Christians today are experiencing the call to a more intimate relationship with God, yet because of the poverty of their previous religious education, they feel totally inadequate to know what direction to go in pursuing a better relationship with God.

God is calling many individuals today to a deeper life of prayer and spirituality. However, most of those who are being called feel very much like babes in the wood when it comes to knowing which direction to go in pursuit of these new goals. They desperately need help and spiritual direction is the name we give to this necessary guidance. A spiritual director is anyone who is capable of giving spiritual guidance to another person. In the past, spiritual direction was often considered the exclusive prerogative of the clergy. However, a study of the history of spiritual direction during these past two thousand years will show us that in no way was this work of spiritual guidance the exclusive domain of the clergy. Anyone, man or woman, who has a correct and in-depth knowledge of the Christian religion, is capable of being a good spiritual director.

St. Bernard of Clairvaux, a famous spiritual director in the Middle Ages, once remarked that anyone directed by himself is directed by a fool. There are a few exceptional persons, especially those who have reached a very high level of faith, who are so open to God that the Holy Spirit is able to guide them adequately on their spiritual journey. However, we should beware of identifying ourselves with these rare exceptions. One of the main advantages of having another person as our spiritual director is that it makes us accountable on a regular basis to another human being. We all know that we are directly accountable to God, but God usually waits until after death before demanding an account of our life. By that time it may be too late for us to make the needed changes in our life.

We need to be accountable at regular intervals throughout our life on Earth. This accountability has to be to another human being. It is a tremendous boost to our efforts to grow spiritually if we have another person on Earth to whom we go regularly once every month or two and admit openly whether we have or have not been faithful to the spiritual resolutions we agreed to fulfill. The first time we admit our failure is tolerable, but it is too embarrassing to have to admit over and over again that we have failed. So either we start being more faithful to our resolutions or we give up spiritual direction.

The more knowledgeable and experienced the spiritual director is in the ways of God and spirituality, the greater help such a person can be to the directee. Therefore, we should look for the person who can be of the greatest help to us on our journey of faith. Just as we make much effort to find the best medical doctor to whom we go when we are physically sick, so we should look for the best spiritual doctor to help us heal our spiritual ailments. So we make what efforts we can to find as good a spiritual guide as is available. Should, in the course of our life, a better director become available, we should not hesitate to change directors.

In view of the great need for spiritual direction in today's world, Christian women and men should feel a responsibility to get the needed training and education to become spiritual directors. Such training is available today in many educational institutions and programs. If we can afford the time and the money, we should attend these programs and learn the art of spiritual direction. On the other hand, should such training not be available, it is possible to follow a program of self-education that can adequately equip most adult Christians to be good spiritual directors. Besides the knowledge and some training, another qualification to be a good spiritual director is that this person is seriously pursuing his or her own spiritual growth. A third qualification to be a good spiritual director is to have good common sense and good judgment. A final necessary qualification is confidentiality that respects the trust the directee places in the director.

In the second chapter of the Book of Genesis, God states that it is not good for a person to be alone. Isolation from others is one of the main obstacles to one's spiritual growth. We need the support of a spiritual friend to enable us to persevere on our journey of faith. Such a friend will prevent us from seriously deceiving ourselves in regard to our hidden faults. Not only are we often in the dark regarding our faults, we are often unaware of the vast potential for good of which we are capable. Having a spiritual director or spiritual friend is one of the best ways to help us overcome our ignorance regarding ourselves. A spiritual friend is especially helpful in times of trouble, when things do not turn out the way we wanted or expected them. We need the presence of another human being to comfort and console us, to hear our anger, our suffering, our disappointment, and to guide us to acceptance.

Countless persons today are looking for a better relationship with God. In order to have a good, grace-filled experience of God, three ingredients are absolutely necessary: God, a human person, and a moment of grace. Actually these three ingredients are always present and available. Why is it then that more people do not have many grace-filled experiences of God? The answer is that a fourth ingredient is needed, a catalyst. In a chemical process the catalyst is that necessary ingredient that brings about the chemical change. Unless the catalyst is present, no chemical change takes place. In our journey of faith toward a deeper union of love with God, the spiritual director acts as a catalyst. Without the presence of the spiritual director, no grace-filled experience of God occurs. If the spiritual director is present and fulfills the proper tasks of spiritual direction for the directee, the moment of grace will not be lost.

Many people today are reluctant to have another human being act as "director" over their spiritual life. They cherish their freedom too dearly to allow another to make serious decisions as those involved in our relationships with God. As a result many persons today prefer to use the term *spiritual friend* instead of *spiritual director.* This is quite satisfactory. As we become more mature spiritually, we need to assume more direct responsibility for our spiritual life. However, regardless of the level of our maturity, all of us need a spiritual friend. Sometimes, this spiritual friendship can be mutual, so that two mature persons can give the needed spiritual help and counseling to one another.

Benefits of Spiritual Direction

There are four basic benefits to be derived from spiritual direction: accountability, objectivity, encouragement, and challenge. During our lifetime we need on a regular basis to be accountable to some other person. Approximately once a month or at least every couple of months we need to reveal to that person how well we have carried out the resolutions of amendment that were mutually agreed on at an earlier meeting. This person is called a spiritual director or spiritual friend.

A second benefit of spiritual direction is objectivity. We all are inclined to be biased in our own favor. It helps to have a third party who can look at our conduct from a more objective and less subjective point of view. Such a person will usually be able to see where we are deceiving ourselves and point out to us the blind spots in our conscience. It does not necessarily mean that the spiritual director is always right and we are always wrong in the judgments made about our conduct. However, an open and honest discussion between the directee and director has a better chance of arriving at the truth than if we trusted only our own insights.

A third benefit is encouragement. When traveling our journey of faith alone, it is easy to become discouraged at our frequent falls. It is a great help to have a trusted friend who will encourage us in times of failure. The more mature and experienced the spiritual friend or director is, the more we will trust their judgment and accept their encouragement. To keep going we need frequent affirmation.

A fourth benefit of spiritual direction is that an experienced and mature director will frequently challenge us to work harder to develop the full potential of good that is present in us. Many psychologists claim that the average person develops only about 20 percent of one's potential for good. If we ever hope to actualize the remaining 80 percent of undeveloped potential, we need someone to challenge us as well as encourage us. We need also a trusted friend who is courageous enough to confront us with the self-deception that we so easily adopt when dealing with our faults and failures. This confrontation needs to be done with great love by someone whom we are convinced is genuinely concerned about our welfare.

If done properly, spiritual direction results in our spiritual growth in the three areas of knowledge, love, and obedience. By knowledge we come to know God and God's revelation more clearly as well as know ourselves and our neighbor's needs more clearly. By God's grace and presence we come to love God, neighbor, and self more dearly. By obedience to the guidance of the Holy Spirit we come to follow our God-given destiny more nearly. To some extent each of us by our own efforts is able to develop these three areas of spiritual growth. However, under the guidance of an experienced and mature spiritual director we can expect faster and greater progress in knowledge, love, and obedience. "To see thee more clearly, love thee more dearly, follow thee more nearly" *(Godspell).*

Purposes of Spiritual Direction

1. To give guidance in two questions: What must I do to be a saint and how do I discern my God-given destiny during my life here on Earth?
2. To discern the Will of God each day.
3. To attain self-knowledge and overcome self-deception.
4. To maintain a balance between opposite poles of reality and truth and thus avoid fanaticism, extremism, exaggeration of one truth to the neglect of other, equally important truths.
5. To foster wholeness, maturity, and sanctity.
6. To make one accountable to another human being on a regular basis.
7. To overcome sloth, procrastination, excessive self-indulgence.
8. To confront and challenge a person to develop fully one's potential.
9. To give encouragement and hope during depression and failure.
10. To affirm and build the self-respect and self-acceptance of directee.

11. To make present God's healing graces.
12. To conquer the world, the flesh, the devil.
13. To recognize and transform one's positive and negative shadows.
14. To become aware of one's masks and self-deceptions.
15. To teach how to redeem one's sinful tendencies.
16. To become detached from power, pleasure, and possessions.
17. To live a simpler lifestyle, cutting back on one's needs and desires.
18. To be more generous in responding to God's movements of grace.
19. To be more open to the guidance of the Holy Spirit.
20. To learn how to pray better and attain a constant union of love between God and oneself.
21. To learn how to use the Bible in prayer and personalize word of God.
22. To be more generous in responding to each day's moments of grace.
23. To overcome pride, envy, greed, gluttony, lust, sinful anger, and sloth.
24. To handle successfully the different crises of one's life.
25. To become the saint God created and destined one to be.

Guidelines for Spiritual Direction

A knowledge of the following things regarding the directee will enable the director to guide a soul on its journey of faith toward holiness. Answers to many of these questions should be found in the spiritual autobiography that the directee is asked to write for the director. Direct questioning or other means will be needed to obtain answers to the other points. It is hoped that by the end of the first year of spiritual direction all of the following questions will have been discussed and covered.

1. How well is the directee working at the four relationships of love: God, neighbor, self, and nature? (Use Personal Growth Plan for this.)
2. How well does the directee understand and participate in the six steps of the journey of faith? (These need to be experienced repeatedly.)
3. What is the degree of self-discipline of the directee?
4. Where is the directee in the seven levels of faith?
5. Where is the directee saying no to God's calls of grace? What are the excessive attachments in the three Ps: possessions, pleasure, power?
6. How intimate is the directee with Jesus Christ and the Gospels?
7. What are the main obstacles to growth in wholeness and holiness?
8. How mature and balanced in regard to humility and trust in God?
9. Where is the directee unbalanced in opposite poles of reality?
10. When did an adult religious conversion first occur? What was its nature? What happened after this first adult experience of God? (A history of the ups and downs of directee's journey of faith will enable director to recognize any unfinished business of past and present problems to address.)
11. How well does the directee fit into the seven-year cycle of crises in life?
12. What present crisis of faith and new decisions need to be made?
13. What particular aspect of the Mission of Christ is directee now being called to accomplish (prophet-teacher, priest-reconciler, servant leader)?

14. What unfinished work remains in the four steps of individuation (authenticity of the ego, significance before God, transparency to others, solidarity)? (See chapter 11.)
15. How open are you to the Holy Spirit and seven gifts of the Holy Spirit?

Nonpsychological Spiritual Direction

Directee: A person seeking a deeper, more intimate relationship with God; no serious or obvious psychological disorder.

Goals:
- Foster union of love with God.
- Develop a Christ-like love of neighbor.
- Achieve a proper, disciplined love of self.
- Bring one's whole life into harmony with God and God's Will.
- Develop an openness to the Holy Spirit.
- Attain a knowledge of and an intimate, loving relationship with Jesus Christ.
- Continue a spiritual growth in God-likeness and Christ-likeness.
- Grow in both personal and liturgical prayer.
- Progress spiritually through seven levels of faith.

Means:
- Pray, fast (self-discipline), give alms (service to others).
- Discern God's Will each day and faithful obedience to it.
- Commit totally to love of God, neighbor, and self.

Method:

- Maintain regular, scheduled accountability.

- Obtain mutual discernment of God's Will.

- Experiment with traditional methods of spiritual growth in order to discover proper method for directee.

- Encourage, affirm, challenge, confront.

Psychological Spiritual Direction (Christotherapy)

Directee: A soul in pain, seeking wholeness and integration of body, mind, soul, emotions; seeking release from psychic pain and deeper union with God.

Goals:

- Achieve wholeness, balance, integration, insight, discernment.

- Alleviate psychic pain, neurosis, fear, insecurity.

- Initiate a proper relationship of love with God, others, self.

- Promote psychological maturity, healing of neuroses.

- Foster individuation: authenticity, significance, transparency, solidarity.

- Discover the riches of personal and collective unconscious.

- Be open to change and emotional growth.

- Develop a strong, self-disciplined ego in proper, harmonious relationship with the inner self.

- Recognize and use the persona, shadow, complexes, and anima/animus in a mature way.

Means:
- Use all possible spiritual and psychological means available.

- Combine prayer and ministry to others with growth in psychological maturity.

- Use a holistic approach.

Method:
- Take directee wherever he or she is and build up self-confidence and encouragement to become mature and whole.

- Gradually shift from psychological needs to the spiritual needs of prayer, love of God, neighbor, and proper love of self.

- Trust in God's mercy, love, forgiveness.

- God is to be loved rather than feared.

Relationship between director and directee: Director is mediator of faith, hope, trust, knowledge, experience, discernment, love.

CHAPTER 3

Actual Process of Spiritual Direction

The director must never come between a soul and God. The director should always think of oneself as a catalyst or midwife who is present in order to facilitate and assist the relationship between God and the directee. The director uses whatever wisdom, insight, experience, and knowledge he or she has in order to help the directee to be more open to the Will of God, more receptive to receiving God's graces, and more generous in responding to God's call. Every soul is unique and different, so there is no one best way to direct every directee. God has his own peculiar way to lead each person on the path of virtue. The director will try to discern what this way is by looking at the fruits of the directee's life. If they have produced the good fruit of growth in faith, hope, charity, humility, and the other virtues recommended in the Sacred Scriptures, the director will know that the directee is on the right path. A good director needs the ability of discernment. The director also needs to be a person of prayer, humble and open to the Holy Spirit, and ready to follow whatever new insights and intuitions that God sends. In other words, let the Holy Spirit be the real director. The human director allows the Holy Spirit to use one's mind, voice, imagination, and intuition to make known to the directee the Will of God.

Each session of spiritual direction should be as spontaneous and informal as possible, trying to make the directee feel comfortable and at ease, yet at the same time aware of the seriousness of the matter at hand. It is good to begin each session with a brief, shared prayer in which both director and directee pray aloud or silently, as each one may choose. The same opportunity for shared prayer should be provided at the end of the session. If the director is a priest, he should give the directee an opportunity to receive the sacrament of Penance. Regardless of who the director might be, it is appropriate to lay hands on the head of the directee and pray for God's blessing.

Normally a spiritual direction session should be no longer than an hour. Anything less than an hour may result in the directee feeling cheated. The first few minutes can be spent in pleasantries, asking how things have been going with the directee, asking about family, home, and work. However, no more than five minutes should be spent in such pleasantries. The rest of the hour should be given to the work at hand, namely, the spiritual growth of the directee, and the conversation must not get sidetracked into nonpertinent topics. Both should be aware that the business of spiritual direction is important and time is valuable and not to be wasted.

Personal Growth Plan

Among the fifty tools that can be used in spiritual direction, it is my conviction that a Personal Growth Plan is the most helpful and most valuable. This growth plan revolves around the basic relationships of love that comprise the whole God-given purpose of why we were created and sent to live our life on Earth. Ideally one should have two Personal Growth Plans, a quarterly one and a daily one. The quarterly one should be renewed approximately once every three months. The daily one needs to be renewed each twenty-four hours.

Quarterly Personal Growth Plan

To develop a quarterly Personal Growth Plan each individual is urged to follow these steps.

1. Center yourself in a quiet, prayerful environment.
2. Reflect on the questions in each of the five areas.
3. Write down those things in each area where you see the need to make some improvement.
4. Select one thing from each of the five areas as your priorities for the next three months.
5. Develop a plan for carrying out these five things.
6. Set a completion date for each of the goals selected.
7. Share your growth plan with a spiritual friend or director.
8. At the end of a chosen period, share your successes and failures with your spiritual friend.
9. Find a way to celebrate your successes.
10. At end of selected period, choose a new Personal Growth Plan and repeat the above process.

First Area: Relationship of Love with God

1. Is the thought of God the first thing that occupies your attention upon awakening in the morning? Does the thought of God frequently occupy you throughout the day? Is your last thought at night before falling asleep centered on God, God's love for you, your love for God? What can you do to focus your attention more often on God during the day?

2. When you happen to awaken during the night, do you turn your attention to God and spend some time in prayer?

3. How much time do you take each day to give thanks to God for all the blessings and graces, not only to you but to others also? Praising God is another way of giving thanks; also reflecting on how you can make some return to God for all his goodness and love.

4. How much time do you give to formal prayer, that is, time that you set aside exclusively for God? Have you seriously considered tithing your waking hours so that you give a tenth of your day to God in prayer, reading the Bible or other spiritual book, reflecting on your relationship with God, trying to make contact with God and making yourself open to his Word, his Will, and his Holy Spirit?

5. How much are the Sacred Scriptures a part of your prayer time each day? How might you make better use of the Bible in prayer?

6. Do you give God some of your prime time each day, time when you are most alert and most free of distractions? Do you pray first and take care of your other duties later, or do you try to finish all your work and put prayer at the bottom of your list of priorities? Where does God fit into your list of priorities?

7. Do you really trust God? Do you realize that God is your best friend, that he is on your side, that he wants only your best interests, your welfare and happiness? Does fear or love predominate your relationship with God? How can you increase your love and trust of God?

8. What can you do to make God more real in your life? Do you see Jesus as a person who is present with you every moment of day and night?

9. How often do you pray with others?

10. When did you experience a special closeness to God? What can you do to recapture or intensify this special closeness to God or Jesus?

Second Area: Relationship of Love with Others

1. What are you doing to love each member of your family?
2. What are you doing to show love for those with whom you work?
3. How can you do more good for others each day?
4. Are you spending quality time each day with your spouse? Children?
5. Is there anyone you have treated unjustly, uncharitably, unfairly, for which you need to make restitution? Reconciliation?
6. Is there anyone who has offended you and whom you need to forgive?
7. What changes do you need to make in your life in order to be of more loving service to others? What are you doing to share your wealth and possessions with the have-nots of the world? How much have you given in charity this year to help the starving, needy people of the world?
8. Do you have close friends with whom you can share your life and to whom you can go for support and they to you?
9. How well do you handle opposition, conflict, disagreement?
10. How much do you pray for others each day?
11. Jesus commands us to love our enemies (Matt 5:43–48). Who are my enemies? How should I love them?

Third Area: Relationship of Love with Your Inner Self

1. Have you a good self-image? Too high or low opinion of self?
2. How self-disciplined are you? What do you need to do to get better self-control of your addictions, desires, passions?
3. How much time and energy do you give to intellectual development?
4. Do you keep too tight a rein on your feelings?
5. Are you making progress in recognizing your unconscious faults?
6. How do you react when someone points out some fault to you?
7. How do you handle loneliness? Sexuality? Anger? Depression?
8. What do you like and dislike about yourself?
9. How well do you react when others compliment you? Criticize you?
10. How well do you know yourself? How authentic are you? Where are you hypocritical and lacking in honesty? How are you deceitful?

Fourth Area: Relationship of Love with Your Body

1. Do you have a proper respect for your body and take good care of your bodily health? If your body was able to speak to you, would it have any complaints about the way you treat it? What would it say to you?
2. What are your eating habits? Do you eat too much? Drink too much? Do you eat the right nutritional things and stay away from the things that are injurious to your health?
3. Do you take sufficient physical exercise each day? Do you give yourself sufficient leisure, rest, recreation?

4. How many hours of sleep do you give yourself each night? Do you stay up too late watching television?
5. Do you smoke? What are you doing to break this habit?
6. How well do you handle stress? What can you do to relieve stress?

Fifth Area: Relationship with the Environment

1. How does your indulgence in certain habits contribute to the decimation of the Earth's resources? How do you waste these resources?
2. How much recycling of things do you presently do?
3. What are you doing to arouse public interest in the environment?
4. What can you do to stop the "rape of Mother Earth?"
5. How can you be more attuned to the beauty, grandeur, fruitful abundance of creation? What are you doing to protect this beauty?
6. How can you spend more time with nature?

Daily Personal Growth Plan

God is love and we were created in the image and likeness of God. The whole purpose of our existence on Earth is to love. This love will be expressed by five relationships of love: love of God, love of other human beings, love of self, love of nature, and love of enemies. Each morning, we should begin the day thanking God for another opportunity to practice love in each of these five areas. Second, we should spend five or ten minutes discerning how we might do a good job today in each of the five areas of love. Third, we need to petition God to give us the grace and help to fulfill the resolutions of love we have made. During the day, we should fill any free moments with gratitude and love of God and with intercessory prayer for our loved ones and all people in need throughout the world. Each evening, we should take a few minutes to review the events of the day, thanking God for the grace to have practiced love in each of the five relationships and asking forgiveness for any failures to love.

I. Love of God:

Head: How can I grow in wisdom and knowledge of God today?

Heart: How can I increase my desires and expectations of God?

Hand: What actions can I do today to express my love of God?

II. Love of other human beings:

What individual persons can I show a special love today?

Is there anyone I need to forgive?

Is there anyone I need to ask forgiveness?

What can I do to reform and help the communities to which I belong?

What are the needs of society that are not being fulfilled?

What God-given talents do I have that might help fulfill these needs?

III. Love of self:

What can I do to develop my inner self today?

What part of my unconscious shadow do I need to make conscious?

How can I maintain a good balance and order in all my activities?

How can I grow in the areas of authenticity, significance, transparency, and solidarity? (See chapter 11.)

What can I do to take good care of my body today?

IV. Love of nature (Earth, environment, creation):

How can I show a love for animals today?

How can I make a wider distribution of food among have-nots of world?

How can I do a better job of preserving the natural resources of the Earth?

What beauties of God's creation can I enjoy today?

V. Love of enemies:

"But I say to you, Love your enemies and pray for those who persecute you,..." (Matt 5:44).

My Own Experience in Directing Others

I always begin with their relationship of love with God, namely their prayer life, to determine how faithful the directee has been to the resolutions expressed at the last session. It is very helpful if these resolutions have been written down. It is advisable to make two copies of one's Personal Growth Plan so that the director can retain a copy. If there is a confidential matter expressed in the growth plan, the director should not keep the second copy in his or her files.

I keep no written records of my directees. I never tape any of the spiritual direction sessions. I consider this to be part of the contract of confidentiality that is necessary between director and directee. I do require each directee to write a spiritual autobiography of at least fifteen or twenty pages giving the story of their journey of faith at least since their teenage years. After reading it I return the autobiography to the directee. I also ask the directee to update this autobiography once each year to determine where there has been progress and where failure.

From the very beginning I insist that both directee and director have complete freedom to terminate the relationship at any time. Frequently the chemistry between the two is not conducive to a healthy spiritual growth. It is possible for either the director or directee to recognize this. For this same reason I insist that the first couple sessions should be on a trial basis to determine if it is indeed God's Will for the establishment of a relationship of spiritual guidance.

In every spiritual direction session I allow the directee to present whatever spiritual problems, questions, or experiences that concerns him or her. This always comes first on the agenda of each session. Let the directee clear his or her mind of all troubles. Otherwise, the directee will not really listen to what the director has to say. After the deck is cleared of all problems, I go immediately to the four areas of the Personal Growth Plan.

What to Talk About at the First Meeting

The director may ask questions to get a reasonably adequate picture of the directee's situation: single, married, children, work, educational background, religious background, age, any previous experience with spiritual direction. If so, how extensive was it, why did it terminate, how well did it go? This will then lead into the important question: Why did you come to see me? What are your present problems? Your needs? Your life's goals? What do you hope to receive? Why did you choose me? How much time, energy, and effort are you prepared to invest in your spiritual growth? How serious are you about your spiritual progress?

If the exercise of spiritual direction is to be successful, the director will need as good a picture as possible of the personal journey of faith of the directee. One of the areas to be shared would be an account of one's original conversion to God and religion. When in one's life did the directee begin to take one's relationship with God as the most serious responsibility in the whole of life? The director will ask if there have been any deep, spiritual, or mystical experiences of God in the directee's life. During the first session the emphasis should be on the positive elements of the directee's relationship with God. A sharing of past sins, failures, and faults can wait until a later session. By emphasizing the positive, the director will set the whole tone for the future relationship between director and directee as well as show the directee the right attitude to maintain toward God. In the first session the director's main interest is to learn the way that God has been working in the directee's life, both in the past as well as the present.

The director will be especially interested in learning exactly what the directee is now doing in the area of prayer. How much time is given to prayer each day? Exactly what does one do during this period of daily prayer? What time during the day does one pray? How satisfying and how successful is the prayer life of the directee? What problems does the directee have in praying? During the first several sessions the primary concern of direction will be to establish a solid, regular program of daily prayer, unless there is some more pressing problem in the life of the directee to be addressed.

If there is time, other topics to be discussed at the first session would be the whole area of ministry and charity toward others. What is the directee now doing in the way of ministering to the needs of others? What problems exist in this area of service to others? Begin with the relationships with immediate members of family of directee (spouse, parents, children, religious community) and then work out to other relationships. How much time, energy, money, possessions are used to help the poor and needy of the world? Are there any serious problems that the directee might have in either past or present relationships with others? This might be the time to inquire about the relationship with parents and others during childhood. Whether or not the directee comes from a family that was dysfunctional will have much bearing on one's present life.

If there is time, ask about habits of self-discipline that the directee is practicing at present: fasting, self-denial, sacrifices of bodily pleasure for sake of some higher good. The director needs to know how self-disciplined or self-indulgent the person is. Unless the directee is really serious about prayer, ministry to others, and self-discipline, the whole effort of spiritual direction will be in vain. Ordinarily a director should not agree to give ongoing direction to a person who lacks seriousness of purpose about spiritual growth in the four relationships of love of God, neighbor, self, and nature.

If there is not sufficient time in the first session to cover all four relationships of love, the director will be content to have a fairly clear picture of the prayer life of the directee. The other relationships of love of neighbor, self, and nature can be postponed until a later session. However, they should be addressed as soon as possible since all four relationships are closely interrelated and interdependent. It is interesting to note that in the Synoptic Gospels, for every one reference to the love of God, there are three references to love of neighbor.

Before ending the first session, the director will talk about a Personal Growth Plan for the intervening time until the next session. The directee will be asked to make a definite commitment to do something toward spiritual growth in each of the areas that have been discussed. The director will take care that the directee does not take on too many commitments. It is better to be successful in one or two small areas rather than to risk discouragement at the failure of some heroic undertaking.

The decision by the director and directee regarding the advisability of continuing the direction need not be made at the first meeting. Both director and directee may want more time to reflect and pray over the experience of the first meeting in order to determine if the chemistry is right between the two of them to give reasonable assurance of success in this work of spiritual direction. Both directee and director should always feel free to terminate the relationship at any time should either of them become convinced that it is not in the best interests of either of them. The spiritual director especially has the responsibility to make a prudent judgment concerning the advisability of continuing or ending the spiritual direction. The director may be presumed to be in the position to make a more objective judgment regarding the success or failure of direction. Directees, however, are also able to discern if the experience is really worthwhile and productive of spiritual growth. One is not always successful in making the right choice of a director the first or second time one tries.

Things to Discuss at Succeeding Sessions

The success or failure regarding the commitments made at the previous session will usually be the first item on the agenda of each meeting. This is where the best decision can be made regarding the seriousness of purpose of the directee. Compassion and understanding of the situation of the directee is necessary but a good spiritual director will be adamant in insisting that the directee be faithful to the commitments agreed on. The director should consider terminating the relationship if the directee consistently fails to live up to the resolutions made. These resolutions should be seen primarily as a self-contract rather than a promise made to God or the spiritual director. This self-contract is shared with the director in order to add the new dimension of accountability that is the key to the success of spiritual direction.

Whatever areas involved in the four relationships of love of God, neighbor, self, and nature that were not covered in the first session should be discussed in the second session. Also, it is good to go over all the things covered in the first session in order to jog the memory of the directee and to give the director the opportunity to add any further details that are important. By the end of the second session, the Personal Growth Plan for the directee will include four areas: prayer, ministry, personal growth, and love of nature.

It is recommended that the directee chose one resolution in each of the four areas and a limited time of not more than three or four months should be set for each resolution made. At each spiritual direction session the directee will report on the progress or lack of progress in each of the four areas of growth. The big difference between this plan and the one recommended above is that it is made for a period of three or four months instead of each twenty-four-hour period.

In the ministry to others, one of the problems that needs to be addressed is the forgiveness of others. Since it is impossible for us to receive God's forgiveness unless we forgive those who have offended us, this forgiveness is an essential element for any authentic spiritual relationship and growth in union of love with God. This forgiveness often needs to be practiced "seventy-seven times," as Jesus suggests in the Gospel (Matt 18:22), if someone has been hurt deeply in the past. Such forgiveness is a necessary part of the healing of memories of past abuses. Even if the person who caused the injury is now dead, forgiveness may still be needed.

All of the subjects that are treated in this book are items to be discussed in succeeding sessions of spiritual direction. One of the main goals of spiritual direction is to attain and maintain a balanced life. The director will constantly be on the lookout for any undue emphasis on one area of spiritual growth to the neglect of other, equally important areas. Although the first session should emphasize the positive attitude toward God, neighbor, and self, the negative side of life needs also to be addressed in succeeding sessions. What are the faults and obstacles in the life of the directee that are preventing growth in sanctity? What needs to be done in order to overcome these obstacles?

The directee should be asked to submit a written autobiography of one's spiritual life. This will not only give the director an overall view of the journey of faith of the directee, but also it will help the directee to see more clearly the actual working of God's grace in one's life. This spiritual autobiography should include ten or twelve of the main stepping-stones of one's spiritual journey. It will also include the major crises one has experienced, the intersections where one had a choice of which road to take. In his book *At a Journal Workshop: Writing to Access the Power of the Unconscious Evoke Creative Ability*, Ira Progoff gives a number of suggestions of possible topics to cover in this autobiography. It should be somewhere between fifteen and twenty typed pages. Once the director has read it, it should be returned to the safekeeping of the directee.

As mentioned, confidentiality and trustworthiness are absolutely essential elements in spiritual direction. If the spiritual director feels the need to consult someone else regarding a problem of the directee, the directee's permission should always be obtained. It is not recommended that the spiritual direction sessions be taped, or that the director should make written notes of what was discussed. If the director feels the need to make such notes, permission of the directee should be obtained.

CHAPTER 4

Qualities of a Good Spiritual Director

What are the qualities needed by anyone who feels called by God to the ministry of spiritual direction? What are the things one should look for when making a choice of which person one might ask to become one's spiritual director? We will try to list the ideal characteristics of a good spiritual director, realizing that it is unrealistic to expect any one person to measure up to all these virtues. At least we can define the goal that every spiritual director should aim to attain. Knowing these ideals will also help a person to make the right choice of which person to ask when there is more than one possible choice. The hope would be that whomever we choose, that person is at least striving to attain these qualities and is making some progress toward attaining them.

What then are the ideal characteristics of a good spiritual director? This person should be a person of prayer who manifests a certain holiness in life and a closeness and intimacy with God; one who is sincerely trying to grow each day in holiness and wholeness. A spiritual director should be a person of experience who has struggled with the realities of life and who has experienced real suffering in life. Ideally such a one should have had the direct experience of failure, of not being able to attain all of one's goals in life, yet humbly accepted this situation.

A spiritual director should be a person of discernment, insight, and perception; a person of vision who can read the writings on the walls of the soul who is being directed—in other words, a person of good intuitive powers. In addition to the intuitive function, the feeling function of the director also needs to be well developed and activated. This enables the director to empathize and relate to the directee on a personal level.

In looking for a director we are looking for a person of learning who is steeped in the scriptures and in the spiritual traditions of the past. The director should have a reasonably good knowledge of the Bible, especially of the Gospels, but also the whole New Testament as well as some knowledge of the Old Testament. The director should be familiar with the recent scholarship regarding the Bible, and aware of the different literary genre or ways of interpreting the scriptures. The director should not be tied down to a literalist, fundamental approach to interpretation of the Sacred Scriptures. The director should know how to use the Bible in one's personal prayer in order to have an intimate relationship with God, and be able to transpose the insights of the Bible to the situations facing us today. St. Teresa of Avila was once asked if she had the choice between choosing a spiritual director who was very holy and one who was very learned, which would she choose? Surprisingly, St. Teresa said that she would choose the very learned person.

A spiritual director should be a person who is able to recognize and follow the inspirations of grace in one's life in order to arrive at the goal to which God is leading each of us. Such an ability implies a total openness to the Holy Spirit, the ability to catch the vibrations of grace needed to guide another soul on the journey of faith.

The spiritual director needs to be someone who will challenge us when it is needed; someone who will help us to grow spiritually and not allow us to remain in our lethargy, sloth, selfishness, self-pity, fear, anger, frustrations, conceit, self-centeredness. We also need someone who will encourage us when that is needed, someone who will affirm us in a very positive way and thus bring out the best in us. St. Francis de Sales remarked centuries ago that you can catch more flies with a spoonful of honey than a barrel full of vinegar.

The spiritual director should be someone who has good common sense and prudence in making balanced decisions. This will prevent the directee from going to extremes and becoming fanatical. The director will know how to tune down the excessive enthusiasm of the directee and thus prevent one from trying to do too much too quickly and then failing completely.

We need someone who truly loves us and is willing to sacrifice oneself for us. We need someone who can be trusted with the secrets of one's soul and know that what is told in direction will not be shared with anyone else. A good spiritual director will be truly concerned about the welfare of others and be willing to give time and energy to helping others. He or she will be convinced of the need of people today to have good guidance and be willing to sacrifice herself or himself for others.

Ideally, a good spiritual director will have a working knowledge of Jungian psychology. This means a knowledge of how to get in touch with one's unconscious and unlock the spiritual treasures that are waiting to be brought into consciousness and put to good use. God dwells in this inner world of the unconscious psyche and often this is the best means available to us to discover God's Will in our regard. If the spiritual director knows the best insights concerning how to attain psychological maturity, this will become another help on our journey of faith toward wholeness and holiness. A knowledge of psychology will help the directee to avoid the pitfalls of transference and projection that can seriously hinder us on the road to sanctity.

A good spiritual director will be someone with strong faith, hope, and trust in God and in God's loving care, someone who is optimistic and hopeful regarding the future. The director needs to be convinced that, with God's help, people will be able to resolve the many problems facing the human race today. This is the opposite of the Deist position that claims that humankind is left alone by God to work out its own problems. This is also opposite to negativity that is like a spiritual cancer in the human psyche. A good spiritual director knows the power of positive thinking and will constantly use this in direction.

A Christian spiritual director should believe in the divinity of Jesus Christ, and is someone who recognizes the validity of the resurrection of Jesus and the future resurrection of all those who die believing in Jesus Christ. This means someone who believes in an afterlife, personal survival after death, and accepts the fact that there is more to life than this earthly existence. We are looking for a person who accepts both the Ten Commandments of the Old Testament and the Sermon on the Mount of New Testament, where Jesus asks much more of Christians than was asked of the people of the Old Testament.

A good spiritual director is one who is willing to live with many mysteries concerning God, the problem of evil, and God's plans concerning the future of the human race and the world. In other words, a good spiritual director is someone who is humble and recognizes our human limitations of knowledge. This means that one must live primarily by faith and trust in God.

The spiritual director must believe wholeheartedly in the free will of human beings, the freedom to accept or reject God's grace. This means the freedom to sin or to practice virtue, the freedom to be saved or to be lost. The director should have experience in dealing with the problems that arise in the life of the average Christian living in today's world. This experience would be for both married and single people in the world as well as people from dysfunctional families, broken homes, adult children of alcoholic parents, single parent families, and so on. Knowing the many problems facing people today, the director will not be so ready to label as "sinful," actions that are wrong but committed without the necessary freedom of will or knowledge and experience that would make them sinful.

A good spiritual director will be seriously interested in becoming a better Christian; one who has been struggling for some time to improve one's personal relationship with God and Jesus Christ. This means that he or she is seriously trying to improve his or her own prayer life and is searching for wholeness and holiness in every aspect of life. Such a person will be humble in regard to one's own gifts, vividly aware of one's total dependence on God, realizing and appreciating the need of prayer and the help of God's grace in order to live and grow spiritually.

The spiritual director needs to be a good listener, to be open to the uniqueness of each individual in order to help that person to recognize the special inspirations of grace present in one's life, and to encourage one to follow such inspirations. The director should be a catalyst who is able to bring God to the directee and bring the directee to God. The director may also be seen as a midwife who assists in the birth of a new relationship with God for the directee. A third image is that of being a physician of souls who provides a suitable environment for the process of spiritual healing to occur in the directee. The spiritual director needs to be sensitive to the subtle movements of the Holy Spirit in the soul of each directee. God moves differently at different periods of each person's life. The director must be alert to the special moments of grace when they occur in the directee's life and call attention to these special graces.

The director is careful not to impose one's own will on the directee but is constantly alert to the voice of God as it is revealed in the life of the directee. The director is careful not to insist too strongly on his or her interpretation of God's Will for the directee, but gently suggests one's insights. If the director's insights are usually correct, in time the directee will learn to give more credence to them. There is such a multiplicity of ethical options facing the sincere Christian today that everyone needs the added insights of a director in order to discern the particular path God is calling one to follow. Without such a director, life can become exceedingly lonely and we can become so totally confused that it is impossible to decide alone which way to go. It is in such moments of frustration that we appreciate the help of a director or spiritual friend.

One of the most important qualities needed by a spiritual director is humility. There is a serious danger of ego inflation whenever anyone engages in the art of spiritual guidance. There is a frequent temptation for the director to try to play God in the life of the directee. John Yungblut, in his book *The Gentle Art of Spiritual Guidance,* calls this the ultimate blasphemy and says that malpractice here is the unforgivable sin against the Holy Spirit. For this reason the director must never forget that one is serving merely as God's instrument in helping the directee get in direct contact with the Holy Spirit. God is always the primary director even though the human director is asked to be a co-creator with God in transforming a soul into the image of God. Yungblut insists that it is only if the director has a full consciousness of the awesomeness of the task will one be able to keep humble and avoid abusing the privilege of being God's helper in sanctifying a soul.

In his book *Companions on the Inner Way: The Art of Spiritual Guidance,* Morton Kelsey insists on the necessity of the director showing an unconditional love for the directee. This love provides the atmosphere so that the love of God for the directee becomes more plausible. This love must stand by the directee in one's ugliness and evil, in times of darkness as well as light. Without love the directee is unwilling to reveal oneself. At the same time this love of the director for the directee frequently results in a psychological transference so that the directee falls in love with the director. Vice versa, the director may fall in love with directee. Therefore proper safeguards must always be present to handle this transference and prevent it from doing harm to one or both parties.

Kelsey suggests five necessary qualities for a spiritual director. First of all, one needs to have a stable religious tradition. Second, one needs to be open to direct mystical experience of God. Third, one needs to have a mature development of one's capacity for critical analysis and thought. Fourth, one needs a good knowledge of the human psyche, how it operates in both the physical and spiritual worlds. Finally, one needs to have learned the art of loving and caring for others. Kelsey says that we do not know how to love instinctively but it has to be cultivated and gradually learned over a long period of time.

Both Kelsey and Yungblut insist that the spiritual director needs to be on a lifelong inner journey, learning to become a true contemplative and mystic. By this they mean that through a cultivation of the gifts of the Holy Spirit one is able to have many direct experiences of God during our life on Earth. These mystical graces may come in many different ways but the result always will be an awareness of God's presence, God's love, and God's call to an ever greater union between God and oneself.

There are any number of helpful tools that a spiritual director can use in leading others to wholeness and holiness. One directee will be helped by one particular tool, while other directees will need a different tool. The more familiar a director is with all available tools of spiritual growth, the better director one will be. The director must be careful not to impose on the directee the particular tool that has best helped the director. Therefore a wise and learned director will be ready to suggest a wide variety of methods of spiritual growth to the directee and then try to discern with the directee which method God has chosen to use in the faith journey of that particular person.

CHAPTER 5

Qualities to Encourage in a Directee

In this chapter I summarize the qualities that the directee should endeavor to put into practice. This will provide a good checklist both for directors and directees to determine how well the directee is fulfilling the requirements for holiness and wholeness. It is impossible for a person to be working at all of these qualities at the same time. Therefore, it is suggested that at each spiritual direction session the directee, with help of the director, should choose one or two of these qualities as the focus of attention for the next month or until the next spiritual direction session. Gradually, over the years of one's life it can be hoped that one will be able to see noticeable progress in all or most of these qualities. There is a great deal of interconnection between the various qualities so that any advance in one area will make it easier for a person to advance in the others.

The first quality to emphasize is a God-centered prayer life. The goal would be for a person to pray constantly, or as Jesus says, to pray always. If possible, every waking moment should be directed to God and God's Will. This does not mean that one is thinking directly about God every moment, but the motive or purpose behind everything one does will be to please God and to do whatever one judges to be God's Will. From the first moment of awakening in the morning, the thought of God and pleasing God will predominate one's attention. One keeps asking oneself, "What does God want, what can I do to please God?" One's whole life is centered in God. The practice of centering prayer is supposed to bring about this kind of a God-centered life. The practice of the presence of God as Brother Lawrence explains it in his book by this same name is another way of living this God-centered life.

Second, one needs to live a service-centered life. Throughout each day one keeps asking, "What can I do to do the most good for the most people?" "How can I use my talents, my energy, my possessions, and my time to help others fulfill their God-given destiny?" One tries to use every opportunity to help others on their journey of faith as well as to help make their life on Earth as joyful and happy as possible. The Gospel says that Jesus went about doing good. The Gospel speaks of Jesus having compassion for the people. At the Last Supper Jesus gave us a new commandment, namely, to love and serve others as he loved and served his disciples when he was on Earth. In his book *Life After Life* (pp. 47, 65), Raymond Moody states that many people who have had an after-death experience relate how they meet a figure of light after death who asks them the question, "What good have you done with your life?"

A third quality would be that of self-discipline. This means self-control, detachment from addictions, and being open to conversion and to change. This means a willingness to give up and let go of whatever God is calling us to sacrifice. Such self-discipline is actually the best way we have of showing a proper love of oneself. It is just the opposite of self-hatred. The self-indulgent person does great harm to oneself for the sake of a momentary pleasure. Only the self-disciplined person is able to activate the tremendous potential for good in one's self.

Another quality to be encouraged is a balanced life. This means the avoidance of fanaticism and extremism. A fully mature person will present a balance between opposite poles of truth and reality. This requires the ability to maintain the needed tension between these opposite poles. This results in a certain amount of stress, but it is this creative tension between opposites that enables one to create and generate new energy, new life. Erik Erikson speaks of this level of maturity as *generativity*.

Some of the opposite poles where a balance needs to be found would be that between work and play, old and new, life on Earth and life after death in heaven, God and neighbor, self and others, God and oneself, justice and mercy, body and soul, conscious and unconscious, and physical health and spiritual health. Part of the necessary balance in life is seen in the four pairs of preferences of the Myers-Briggs Type Indicator. These balances are between extroversion and introversion, sensing and intuition, thinking and feeling, and judging and perceiving.

Maintaining this balance requires a great deal of stress and yet it is this very tension that is creative of new truth, new grace, new energy, and new insights. In order to maintain such a tension and balance between opposite poles, one must find a way to experience relief from stress. This can be accomplished through physical exercise, sleep, play, leisure. By working with the hands in gardening, woodwork, or needlework, one is able to maintain the balance between opposites without undue stress. One needs to work at this throughout one's life on Earth.

Another important quality to encourage in the directee is a positive attitude toward God, others, oneself, the future, and the world. There is so much negativity in the world today so that negativity has become a contagious, psychic disease. One needs constantly to struggle against having a negative attitude. One of the clear signs of the practice of love as well as a sign of maturity is for a person to have a positive attitude of love. Instead of being judgmental in a negative way toward God, self, others, the world, or the future, a mature, loving person will always have a positive, hopeful, optimistic attitude.

Another quality needed by a mature person is the ability to change, to be converted, and to give up the old attachments when it becomes clear that it is best to move on to something new and different. We must never be wholly satisfied with the present situation. We must remain open and ready to improve the present, always growing, changing, and developing, always in process. While holding on to all that is good in the past, we must be able and ready to cast overboard whatever is no longer of value from the past or present. Such an attitude requires both wisdom and courage. We need wisdom in order to know when it is necessary to leave the present and the past; when it is necessary to stand alone and disagree with others. This is part of the experience of crucifixion and the cross that Jesus says we must take up daily and follow him. Thus one is able to separate the wheat from the chaff, both of old and new. Besides wisdom, such openness requires much courage as well as deep inner faith, trust, and hope in God.

Another quality to encourage in the directee is a seriousness of purpose, a total commitment to God, a total surrender to God's Will. Like Jesus one can hope to be able truthfully to say, "And the one who sent me is with me; he has not left me alone, for I always do what is pleasing to him" (John 8:29). This seriousness of purpose needs to be balanced with a good sense of humor that enables one to laugh at oneself and one's mistakes and foibles. One must not take oneself too seriously and be able to take a joke as well as give one. The more we know about God, the more we realize God's sense of humor when he so often makes his friends eat their own words to their own chagrin. With a good sense of humor one is able readily to admit one's mistakes, ignorance, and failures. If we are ever to reach holiness and wholeness, we will often discover that we have taken the wrong road and have ended up in a blind alley. Instead of stubbornly persisting in going forward, we need humbly to admit our error, turn around, and come back and look for a new road. All of this comes from a deep humility, a realization that "I am not God and therefore I am not totally responsible for the world today." We must trust in God to take care of his creation. At the same time, we remain willing to do our part, no matter how small our contribution might be.

Another quality to be encouraged in the directee is tolerance for those who happen to see things differently from ourselves. We must be willing to live with others who have a different worldview, a different way of looking at God, the world, and themselves. We must realize that none of us has a total grasp of the truth. Others often have an insight into a truth that is still hidden from us. For even the wisest person on Earth, there is still considerably more such a person does not know versus what one actually knows. At the same time one should not be wishy-washy in submitting to the opinions of others. One needs to stick by one's convictions regarding the truth while being open to any new insights others may have to offer. This means that we should be good listeners and not try to dominate the conversation with our pet theories and ideas. We must be willing to stop our own conversation the moment we see that a companion wishes to speak. If one's thoughts are important enough, there will be a later opportunity to present them. We must be constantly open to the rights of others and humble and loving enough to give them an opening when they desire to speak. Tolerance for others means a respect for the opinions, convictions, and beliefs of others. We must be willing to live and let live and not pass negative judgment on others' opinions.

When we are able to tolerate differences in others and live at peace with these differences, we will be ready to compromise secondary issues in life while holding on to our primary convictions. It takes much wisdom to be able to make the right decision regarding what is primary and what is secondary in our life. It is safe to presume that most issues are secondary and not too many issues are really primary. Such willingness to compromise is necessary in order to reach a consensus in the really essential things in life.

One of the very first desires to encourage in a directee is the desire to grow in holiness and wholeness. This deep, sincere desire to have a growing intimacy with God and Jesus Christ and a loving relationship with others should be so great that one is willing to make any sacrifice in order to attain it. God, in turn, loves us so much that he will do all in his power to help us fulfill our desires for holiness.

The four qualities of individuation that Carl Jung recommends are also qualities to be encouraged in every directee. They are authenticity, significance, transparency, and solidarity. (These qualities are explained in chapter 11.) Another quality to encourage in the directee is the ability to handle suffering, pain, and failure. One must learn to rise above one's failures and not become depressed or discouraged. One needs to learn how to suffer pain with tolerance and patience. We need to accept our creatureliness and realize that pain and suffering are necessary adjuncts to growth in maturity and holiness. Thus we are able to handle the negative things in life in a positive, loving way.

Another quality to encourage is a love of freedom, a desire to be detached from all addictions, so that we can be totally open to God's love and God's Will. Such openness to

God results in a freedom from fear, be it fear of death, pain, failure, opposition. This is possible only if we have a deep, child-like faith and trust in God. We need total, blind trust in God's power, goodness, wisdom, love, and faithfulness to his Word.

CHAPTER 6

Six Steps of Our Journey of Faith

All of life is a journey toward a future goal. Ultimately it is a journey toward death and life after death. More immediately it is a journey toward a fuller experience of the kingdom of God on Earth. Another way of expressing it is that it is a journey toward holiness and wholeness, toward spiritual and psychological maturity. Leon Bloy states that there is only one tragedy and that is not to be a saint. Unless we attain true sanctity, our life on Earth is a failure. The goal of sanctity is within reach of every human being, provided we cooperate with the grace of God that is given us each day. In order to reach our life's goals, we need to make continual progress on our journey of faith. All of life is an experience that is either progressing or regressing. We cannot remain in one spot very long, otherwise we begin slipping back. It is like trying to drive a car on an icy hill. As long as we keep moving forward we are able to progress to the top of the hill. However, if we stop, we may have to slide back to the bottom in order to get a fresh start.

In the course of our journey of faith there are certain steps that need to be repeated again and again before attaining our goal of holiness and wholeness. Another image that will help us to visualize our journey is that of a spiral staircase that keeps circling back again and again toward the same direction, but always at a higher level. The steps of our spiritual journey can, for the most part, be included under the following six headings:

1. Listening to God's Call
2. Experiencing a Faith Conversion
3. Entering into a Covenant of Faith with the Risen Lord Jesus
4. Celebrating the Covenant with the Faith Community
5. Receiving the Consolations of the Holy Spirit
6. Receiving a Commission to Share our Faith with Others

We might think of these six steps as the six "Cs." The first step is God's *call* or *challenge* or *communication*. The second step is our response of *conversion* or *change of direction* in our life. The third step is entering into a *covenant* of faith with the Risen Lord Jesus. We might call this third step a mutual *contract* we make with God and the Lord Jesus whereby each of us makes a total *commitment* of our life to each other. The fourth step is the ever-repeated *celebration* of the *covenant* in Eucharist with the *community* of believers. The fifth step is receiving the *consolations* of the Holy Spirit. The sixth step is the *commission* from God to share our faith with others.

In spiritual direction the directee will be encouraged to experience these six steps again and again throughout one's life on Earth. Actually it is possible to be experiencing some or all of these steps at the same time, but in reference to different tasks and aspects of holiness and wholeness. The director will especially urge the directee to keep repeating the first step of listening to God's call of grace. Before we can answer this call, we need to hear clearly the particular challenge God is calling us to accomplish at this particular stage of our journey of faith. This challenge of God's call of grace may change and vary even from one day to the next. Therefore the directee needs to be alert and actively listening to whatever God is trying to communicate. Sometimes God is merely affirming us in our present efforts, urging us simply to keep going in the direction we are now going. At other times God will be calling us to change the direction of our life, perhaps to let go of something to which we are deeply attached and go in a new direction with our life. We call this a "slaying of our darlings" or a sacrifice of our little Isaacs. Whatever the call might be, our response should be a positive yes.

Listening to God's Call

God speaks to us in many ways, but for Christians the primary way is through the words of the Bible. Both the Old and New Testaments give us God's Word, but this Word has to be transposed and interpreted so that it has meaning for our particular situation today. How do we know that we are interpreting the Word of God in the Bible correctly? This is indeed a problem since we know that countless people have misread and wrongly interpreted the Word of God to their own destruction. In the words of the author of the Second Epistle of Peter: "There are some things in them [his letters] hard to understand, which the ignorant and unstable twist to their own destruction, as they do the other scriptures" (2 Pet 3:16). In the Sermon on the Mount, Jesus gives us the basic rule for discerning whether we are interpreting the words of Bible correctly: "Thus you will know them by their fruits" (Matt 7:20). This means that ultimately we must trust our common sense and good judgment, which involves a real risk. In case of doubt or uncertainty, we should consult others who are wiser than ourselves. One of the benefits of spiritual direction is to be able to submit our interpretation of scripture to another person in order to check the validity of its meaning. However, there are countless passages in the Bible that can be clearly understood even by the least educated person.

God also speaks to us in many other ways, through the written or oral words of others, through our conscience, our common sense, our experience. God reveals his Will to us through divine providence and the events of our daily life. God frequently speaks to us through our dreams. We might say that God is communicating with us every moment of the day. Our problem is to keep open these lines of communication with God rather than tune his voice out of our consciousness. A spiritual director should make sure that the directee daily tries to communicate with God in order to discern God's call of grace. These divine calls will vary in intensity from day to day. At times God's call is very strong and insistent, at other times it is very gentle and patient. A spiritual director will help one to discern those special times of grace that the Bible calls *kairos*. They frequently come during a time of crisis or tension when we have to make a choice between two or more possible ways to go with our life.

Frequently, God's call of grace contains a challenge to change the present direction of our life in order to take a higher road. God loves us as we are, sins and faults and all, but we can be sure that God would like to see every one of us somewhat better than we now are. Our goal of perfection, wholeness, maturity, sanctity is a goal that we never totally attain here on Earth. There is always more to be done than what we have already accomplished. One of the main purposes of spiritual direction is to help us discern the challenges of the new direction to which God is calling our life, and then to assist us to respond to this call of grace as generously as possible.

It helps us to discern God's call if we use a notebook or spiritual journal to write down what we think God is saying to us

Jesus and the Christian community of faith, this celebration needs to be done in a community setting. The normal and traditional way the community of believers has celebrated the covenant during these past two millenniums is the weekly parish Mass. All the other sacraments are also celebrations of the different aspects of the Christian covenant, but it is the weekly Eucharist that is the high point as well as the basic foundation that undergirds our community covenant with the risen Lord Jesus. Our covenant has both a vertical and horizontal dimension. We relate to God and Jesus on a personal, one-to-one basis as well as a community of believers that recognizes the presence of Jesus whenever it gathers two or more members in his name.

Both individually as well as communally there is a basic spiritual need to express and experience our faith, hope, and love toward Jesus and God. Without both the personal and community expression of a covenant relationship of love with God, this relationship will wither and die. Just as so many other aspects of our life on Earth revolve around a weekly schedule, a weekly liturgical gathering of the faith community is essential to its survival. Ideally, the weekly eucharistic liturgy should be the peak moment of our journey of faith. If this does not occur, this is proof that somewhere we have short-circuited the covenant process. The fault may lie with the individual or with the whole community. If there is no authentic personal commitment of love to Christ by the individual, then participation in the Sunday Eucharist is a hypocritical farce. If there are no ongoing faith community experiences of the covenant, it is next to impossible to expect the one-hour of the weekly Eucharist to be an experience of the presence of Jesus Christ. Much homework is required both individually as well as communally in order to have a good celebration of our covenant with Jesus and God.

Spiritual direction must never be limited to the vertical dimension of the individual directee's relationship with God and Jesus. Since we relate to God both as an individual and as a community, the directee needs to report on both of these relationships. What has the directee done since the last spiritual direction session to foster the life of the whole community of believers? What contribution is the directee making in order to help make the Sunday Eucharist a peak experience of faith for everyone?

The Eucharist gathers in one great moment of grace the whole history of salvation, past, present, and future. By means of the four symbols of community, word, meal, and cross, the whole paschal mystery of Christ is made present so that all those at Mass may join their life to the life, death, and resurrection of Jesus. In each Eucharist we renew our baptismal commitment to God and Jesus both as an individual and as a community of believers. Jesus makes himself present and available to us just as he did to sinners, sufferers and other people during his public life in Galilee. He respects our freedom and will never force himself on us. If we generously open our hearts in loving commitment to God's Will, Jesus will become present to us in each Eucharist.

Receiving the Consolations of the Holy Spirit

If we successfully carry out the previous four steps of our journey of faith, we can expect as a matter of course the consolations of the Holy Spirit. St. Paul calls them the fruits of the Holy Spirit: love, joy, peace, patience, kindness, generosity, faithfulness, gentleness, purity (Gal 5:22–23). We may also add the gifts of the Holy Spirit, both those general gifts (Isa 11:2–3) and the special gifts that Paul describes in the twelfth chapter of First Corinthians.

We know that it was through the power of the Holy Spirit that Jesus of Nazareth was able to carry out his mission on Earth. He assured his apostles after his resurrection that they would receive an outpouring of the Holy Spirit that would enable them to perform even greater works than Jesus had done (John 14:12–18). These are the consolations of the Holy Spirit that we can expect on our journey of faith. St. Teresa of Avila once remarked that all the way to heaven is heaven too. It is due to the consolations of the Holy Spirit that we are able here on Earth already to experience something of the happiness we will receive in heaven.

In the Acts of Apostles, the people asked Peter what must they do. He replied that they must be converted and be baptized and then they will receive the gift of the Holy Spirit (Acts 2:38). Receiving the gifts of the Holy Spirit is a direct result of our carrying out the first four steps of our journey of faith. If we listen carefully to God's calls of grace, experience a true conversion of our heart to God, enter into a lifelong commitment and covenant with the Lord Jesus, celebrate frequently that covenant of faith with the believing community, then surely we can expect an effusion of the gifts, fruits, and consolations of the Holy Spirit in our life here on Earth. Actually, we need the constant help of the Holy Spirit in order to carry out the first four steps of our journey of faith, but frequently this help is given secretly without our being aware of its source. It is usually only in the later stages of our faith journey that we have visible, tangible manifestations of the Holy Spirit in our life. Frequently, God will give a taste of the consolations of the Holy Spirit at the very beginning of our faith journey in order to wean us away from the pleasures of this world. Then there often results a long period of dryness and cold, hard faith before experiencing a new effusion of the consolations of the Holy Spirit. However, if we are faithful to our faith commitments, these consolations will surely come, even in the midst of physical suffering.

Among the consolations of the Holy Spirit will be those general and special, charismatic gifts that we need in order to carry out our mission and destiny on Earth. The spiritual director should encourage every directee to have a special devotion to the Holy Spirit. Jesus told his apostles that it was better for him to leave them, "for if I do not go away, the Advocate will not come to you; but if I go, I will send him to you" (John 16:7). We need the help of the Holy Spirit in order to do our God-appointed work on Earth. Just as the Holy Spirit turned around the whole life of Jesus from the private carpenter of Nazareth to the Messiah who redeemed the world, that same Spirit can turn around our life from an ordinary nobody to someone who is able with the help of this same Holy Spirit to change the world.

Receiving a Commission to Share Our Faith with Others

In Psalm 116:12 the author asks, "What shall I return to the Lord for all his bounty to me?" Every one of us has received abundant graces from the Lord during our journey of faith. The best return we can make to the Lord is to pass on to others the faith and gifts we have received. This is our way of expressing gratitude to God for his generosity to us. In the Gospels Jesus frequently urged his apostles to pass on to others what they had received: "As the Father has sent me, so I send you" (John 20:21); "Go therefore and make disciples of all nations" (Matt 28:19); "You received without payment; give without payment." (Matt 10:8).

In spiritual direction, there is the danger that the directee becomes so concerned about one's personal growth in sanctity that one is tempted to neglect one's responsibilities to others. This is why the second area of the Personal Growth Plan is important and essential to everyone's journey of faith. We will never be successful in our faith journey if we neglect our responsibilities of ministry to others. In the twenty-fifth chapter of Matthew's Gospel, Jesus assures us that he will consider as done to him whatever we do or fail to do to our neighbor. Jesus says that this is how everyone will know whether we are his disciples, by the love we show to one another. The whole New Testament is an expanded explanation and example of this sixth step of our faith journey.

Archimedes once said that with a solid fulcrum and a lever long enough, he could lift the world! We have the fulcrum and two levers by which we can lift the world. The fulcrum is Jesus Christ and the two levers are prayer and action. Regardless of the situation in which we find ourselves, it is possible to make use of each of these levers. The action may be as simple as smiling and bringing a bit of cheer to another person. Prayer does not require words but simply a desire that God will bless another. Norman Vincent Peale has written of the power of positive thinking. A positive attitude toward God, others, ourselves, the world, and the future is another lever by which we can lift the world out of its present negativity.

The life of Jesus on Earth was cut short before he was able to finish the task of establishing the kingdom of God on Earth. It is now up to us, his disciples, to finish the work that Jesus began. Jesus assures us that we will not be alone but that the same Holy Spirit who assisted him will always be present to help us. We are all that God has to carry out the work of the kingdom on Earth. We are the hands and tongues and feet of Christ's mystical body who have been given the task of bringing about the kingdom of God on Earth. People today need hope, need to touch the garments of someone who really believes and has hope. Regardless of our situation, there are persons who need us, who will never know Christ's merciful love unless we tell them about it. We must not allow past failures to discourage us. Much of the good we do for others will never be known until after we die. Frequently what seems from outward appearances to be a failure is used by God to bring many graces to others. One of the main tasks of the spiritual director is to encourage the directee to keep trying, regardless of any apparent lack of success in one's ministry. Also, the regular accountability to the director of one's ministry to others contributes much to perseverance.

CHAPTER 7

Three Obstacles to Grace and Their Remedies

The Three "Ps": Possessions, Pleasure, and Power

Traditionally the three great obstacles on our journey of faith have been called the world, the flesh, and the devil. I would prefer to speak of them as the three Ps: *possessions, pleasure, and power.* All three of these are creations of God and therefore are good, as long as they are kept in their proper place. The problem is that they are so good and attractive that we have a tendency to idolize and worship them. Instead of seeing them as the limited, created good they actually are, we are tempted to make them into absolute goods and thus they replace God as the ultimate goals of our life. We make a god out of a limited good and become guilty of idolatry in our attitude toward it.

Possessions, pleasure, and power offer us a limited security in a very insecure world. Actually insecurity is a necessary condition of life on Earth. It is an essential element of being a creature. However, it is not at all comfortable to be insecure. Therefore, we are constantly on the lookout for anything that can give us a feeling of security. Faith and trust in God are meant to be our ultimate security on Earth. However, when we are lacking this trust in God, we have a tendency to look for anything on Earth that seems to offer a solution to our insecurity. Money or possessions offer a limited security to our earthly life. Therefore, it easily becomes the number one priority in our life. The more money and possessions we can call our own, the more secure we imagine we will be. Bodily pleasure is a second way of gaining more security on Earth. If our body is content with pleasure, we no longer feel insecure. Third, the possession of power over others, over nature, over ourselves, over the future, and over the world can easily become an idol that we worship. If we have power, we no longer feel weak and insecure. Another word for power is *freedom,* the freedom to do whatever we choose to do. Still another word for power is *pride* whereby we exalt our own freedom above the freedom of God and make our will supreme rather than God's Will. By means of one or more of these three Ps, we attempt to attain a false, earthly security rather than find our security in God.

It is interesting to note that the three Ps involve the three basic relationships around which our whole life on Earth revolves. Pleasure has to do with ourselves, especially our bodies. Possessions have to do with our relationship with our neighbor. Power has to do with our attitude toward God. When we worship power, we are attempting to steal from God the omnipotence he enjoys and make ourselves into an absolute power. When we worship pleasure and make it one of our supreme goals in life, we have made a little god out of our body. When we worship possessions and make the acquisition of money and earthly goods the supreme goal of life, we will of necessity fail in our duties of love and service to our neighbor.

The three temptations of Jesus during his sojourn in the desert may also be seen as an attempt by Satan to get Jesus to make an absolute good out of possessions, pleasure, and power. The first temptation to turn the stones into bread was a subtle way of tempting Jesus to use the miraculous powers he now

THREE OBSTACLES TO GRACE AND THEIR REMEDIES

possessed to satisfy his own bodily pleasure. Actually these God-given powers were to be used only to help others and carry out his ministry as the Messiah. The second temptation, according to the Gospel of Luke, was Satan's offer to give Jesus possession of all the Earth in exchange for Jesus' worship of Satan. The worship of Satan seems to be the price we must pay when we make acquisition of money and earthly possessions the supreme goal of our life. The third temptation was a subtle appeal to the power that Jesus now enjoyed over nature by floating down into the Temple Square from the highest pinnacle of the temple. This would have been a wrong use of Jesus' power and an act of pride on Jesus' part by showing off his superhuman powers. Therefore, Jesus rejects this as well as the other suggestions from Satan. No matter how much power we may have it is never to be used selfishly but only in accord with the Will of God. The same is true of pleasure and possessions.

One of the main tasks of a spiritual director is to help a directee become aware of the presence of all three of these obstacles to grace throughout one's life on Earth. It is not advisable to talk about the obstacles in the first or second session of spiritual direction unless the directee brings up the subject. However, by the third session a thorough discussion is recommended of how the directee has handled these three obstacles in the course of one's whole life. This will give the director some good insights regarding the future direction the directee should go.

Forewarned is forearmed. Satan is very clever in the many subtle ways we are tempted to exaggerate the importance of possessions, pleasure, and power in our present life. Since each of these three Ps is actually something good and created by God for our use and benefit, it is easy to be deceived in our pursuit of these three worthwhile goals of life. Instead of keeping them as limited goals in life, we are often tempted to make them into absolute goals around which our life revolves. We may put one or more of them ahead of God in our daily life and thus we become guilty of idolatry or worship of false gods.

It can be safely presumed that every directee has been tempted to idolize possessions, pleasure, and power. The source of every human sin can be traced to an exaggerated emphasis and value placed on one or the other of these three Ps. This becomes especially apparent if instead of power, we use pride as the third P. St. Paul says that the love of money is the root of all evil (1 Tim 6:10). It would probably be more correct to say that pride or the excessive love of self is the origin of all sins. The seven capital sins are simply different ways of exaggerating the place of possessions, pleasure, and power in our life. Greed and envy involve our attitude toward earthly possessions. We are greedy when we exaggerate the value of earthly goods. We are envious when we begrudge others having more of this world's goods than we possess. Gluttony, lust, and sloth are different ways our pursuit of pleasure goes astray. Gluttony exaggerates the value of food and drink, lust does the same for sexual pleasure, and sloth carries to extreme the desire for ease and comfort. Pride and anger are concerned with power. Pride is present when we put our desires and our will ahead of God's Will. Sinful anger is present whenever we desire to do violence to anyone who poses a threat to our freedom and power.

In every spiritual direction session after the introductory sessions, the director will inquire regarding any problems, temptations, struggles, and failures of the directee in each of the three Ps. Has there been an overemphasis on earthly possessions, bodily pleasure, or the selfish use of power or freedom? Without being personally aware of it, we often find ourselves tempted to make one or other of these three created goods an ultimate goal of life. One of the tasks of a spiritual director is to make the directee more consciously aware of the presence and attraction of possessions, pleasure, and power in one's daily life. Because they are so attractive to us, they easily become our masters. We begin to serve them as our gods instead of the true God. This is such a total distortion of truth that when we make any one of the three Ps into absolute goals in our life, they cease to be good and become evil. Because there is so much energy behind each of these three values, as ultimate goals they take on the personality of evil spirits. These evil forces pose a constant threat to our eternal salvation as well as our earthly welfare. When we absolutize any one of these three limited values, we become possessed by their evil energy. A popular term today for such evil possession is *addiction*. We become addicted to possessions, pleasure, or power. Every sin and evil in the world today can be traced to our addiction to one or the other of these three Ps. Only God and God's Will are to be loved absolutely. We must never love any created good or any creature in an absolute, unlimited way.

The Three Remedies

In the Gospel, Jesus told his apostles that there are certain evil spirits that can be cast out only by prayer and fasting (Matt 17:21). We need to add almsgiving to prayer and fasting and say that the only way to be delivered from a slavery or addiction to possessions, pleasure, or power is by the practice of the three remedies of prayer, fasting, and almsgiving. Through prayer we acknowledge our dependence on God's power rather than our own power. Through fasting we bring under control our attraction for sensual pleasure. Through almsgiving we become detached from an excessive love of money and possessions. Our whole Christian tradition has constantly urged us to practice prayer, fasting, and almsgiving. Jesus speaks of all three of these remedies in the sixth chapter of St. Matthew's Gospel. Traditionally these have been the three practices that every

Christian is urged to carry out each day of Lent. Actually, these three practices should be recommended as daily practices during the whole year. Like the three Ps, these three remedies involve the three relationships of love around which our whole life should revolve. Prayer deals with having a good, loving relationship with God. Fasting is directed toward a proper, balanced love of self. Almsgiving refers to all our duties of love of neighbor.

Prayer

Prayer enables us to keep the temptation to power under control. When we pray we recognize God as the only one with absolute power and we submit our will and freedom to God's Will. We might define prayer as anything that helps our relationship of love with God. As such it does not require words or any special form or method. The goal of our prayer life is to have the thought and desire of God always before us every waking moment of our life. Brother Lawrence's book *Practice of the Presence of God* is a good example of our life's goal for prayer.

The accomplishment of a total union with God is the work of our whole lifetime on Earth. It is a task to which we need to address our attention every single day of our life. It is recommended that in every spiritual direction session the first question addressed to the directee will be, "What about your prayer life?" The directee will be asked to give an account of what resolutions were made in the Personal Growth Plan that involved prayer and one's relationship of love with God. By making this the first concern of spiritual direction, the directee will begin to realize that this must always come first every day of one's life. We will never be able to carry out our duties of love of neighbor and a proper love of self unless we have the necessary help from God that comes through prayer. Gerald G. May has written an excellent book, *Addiction and Grace: Love and Spirituality in the Healing of Addictions,* in which he shows that it is impossible to overcome our addictions without the grace of God.

The most important result of each experience of prayer is an increase in the virtue of humility. By humility we mean a constant, conscious recognition of our total dependence on God and our total helplessness as a creature apart from God. *Humility* is a synonym for authenticity and truth and it is the basic foundation on which all the other virtues depend. It addresses the whole problem of power and personal freedom and is the direct opposite of pride and the exaggerated love of one's own power. Humility and prayer are so closely connected that it is impossible to have humility without prayer and impossible to pray well without humility.

The reason why possessions, pleasure, and power can so easily take hold of our souls is that each of them promises a certain security in this very insecure world. Prayer is the only antidote that will counteract the poison in our system that results from an excessive concern with possessions, pleasure, or power. This is true because a direct result of prayer is an increase of trust in God. Such trust in God is the only real, lasting security that is possible here on Earth. In prayer we freely choose to trust God's power. When we neglect to pray, we choose to trust our own power to decide and to act. God indeed has shared with us some of his power and freedom. But these are limited gifts and we are guilty of pride when we choose to act as though our human freedom was an absolute power. Pride is therefore a form of idolatry. We make a god out of our power to choose, our freedom to act. We put more trust in ourselves than we do in God. By prayer we choose to center our life in God.

Prayer had such an important place in the life of Jesus on Earth. He spent entire nights in prayer. His whole life was centered in God, his Heavenly Father. He trusted in the power of

God rather than his own human powers. He insisted that his disciples have a similar trust in God and Jesus taught them how to express this trust in God through prayer. The Lord's Prayer is an example of such trust in God. Jesus' temptation to cast himself down from the pinnacle of the temple was a temptation to trust his own human power as an absolute power instead of recognizing its limitations. Jesus' reply to this temptation was, "Do not put the Lord your God to the test" (Matt 4:7; Luke 4:12). Each day we fail to pray, each time we give into the temptation of pride, each time we trust in our own freedom and power rather than in God, we put God to the test. In other words, we tempt the Lord our God.

Fasting

Fasting is the generic term for all those acts of self-discipline by which we bring under reasonable control our desires for sensual pleasure. When used specifically, *fasting* refers to moderation in the use of food and drink. In the Gospel, Jesus puts fasting on a par with prayer as a necessary means to rid ourselves of evil. When the apostles asked Jesus why they were unable to cast out an evil spirit, Jesus replied that there were certain evil spirits that could be cast out only by prayer [and fasting] (Matt 9:29). A more modern word for fasting is *self-discipline*. It refers to keeping the proper balance in all of our desires and appetites, especially the desire for bodily pleasure. It does not mean that we should torture ourselves or that God enjoys seeing us suffer or being miserable and unhappy. God wants us to enjoy life on Earth but for this to happen, everything must be done in moderation. Pleasure is one of God's creations for our benefit. However, like possessions and power, the pursuit of earthly pleasure is meant to be a limited good. When we make pleasure an absolute good we make a god out of it. St. Paul says that such persons make their belly their god (Phil 3:19).

The very first temptation Jesus had during his sojourn in the desert was to gratify his hunger by turning stones into bread. Jesus' response to Satan was, "One does not live by bread alone" (Matt 4:4). Jesus is not condemning the pleasures of food. Jesus enjoyed eating and drinking to the extent that his enemies accused him of being a glutton and a drunkard. Rather, Jesus is reminding us that bodily pleasure is a limited good and not an absolute one. Because the attraction toward sensual pleasure is so powerful, we need to place a restraint on its enjoyment. The goal of fasting and self-discipline is to establish a proper attitude of love toward ourselves and our own needs. The ideal is to make use of bodily pleasure only to the extent that God wills it for us. To discern God's Will we can study the example of Jesus in the Gospels and then by prayer and experience decide what is proper for our present situation.

The third area of the Personal Growth Plan concerns the proper relationship with our inner self and bodily care. After love of God and love of neighbor, the third most important concern in spiritual direction is a proper love of self. Therefore, in every session of spiritual direction the directee should be asked to give an account of what has been done in the two areas of bodily care and inner growth. This is accomplished by means of self-discipline or fasting.

Almsgiving

As a generic term, *almsgiving* is synonymous with love of neighbor. It is much broader than merely giving money or possessions to the poor. We need to broaden our understanding of possessions to include all the gifts and blessings of our life: our time, our talents, our energies, our intelligence, our experience, as well as our material possessions. Almsgiving is concerned with all our relationships with others, and if it is practiced properly, it will prevent us from making a god out of any of our possessions and blessings. By almsgiving we willingly share our gifts with the less fortunate of the world. We recognize that we are merely stewards of the possessions that happen to be listed in our name. One day we will have to render an account to God whether we have used all of these gifts to do the greatest possible good to everyone. We have an obligation to take care of our own personal needs as well as those of our family and dependents. But it is against justice for us to have luxuries and an overabundance of the goods of this world while others starve and are deprived even of the barest necessities. By almsgiving we try to bring about a balance between the haves and the have-nots of the world. If it is practiced generously, we will never make a god out of money or any of the things of this world.

In the Personal Growth Plan the second area of concern is our relationship of love with others. Another name for this would be our ministry to others. After inquiring about prayer and our relationship with God, the second area of concern in each spiritual direction session will be this area of ministry and loving service to others. St. John insisted that it is impossible to love God unless we are also doing all in our power to show love to all our neighbors (1 John 4:20). Jesus says that our charity toward our neighbor will be the telltale sign by which we will be known as his disciples (John 13:35). The goal of almsgiving is to fulfill as perfectly as possible the new commandment of love of neighbor that Jesus gave to his disciples at the Last Supper. "I give you a new commandment, that you love one another. Just as I have loved you, you also should love one another" (John 13:34). Webster's dictionary defines *alms* as "something given freely to relieve the poor." If we think of every human being as being poor and needy, then *almsgiving* is a good word to describe all that is involved in loving others as Jesus loved his disciples.

The purpose of almsgiving is to bring under control the very legitimate desire for possessions that God has implanted in our nature for the sake of self-survival. However, like the desires for pleasure and power, the desire for possessions has a tendency to want to become an absolute value instead of a limited good. When we give into this temptation, we make an idol out of our earthly possessions. The love of money and the things money can buy is at the root of much of the evil in the world today. According to Luke's Gospel the price to pay for making possessions the supreme goal of life is the worship of Satan (Luke 4:6–7). Our American culture seems to have made money and earthly possessions the supreme goal of life. We are willing to go to war in order to protect our American way of life. Living in such a culture, each directee is bound to be somewhat contaminated by this excessive regard for money and the things money can buy. The spiritual director will make sure to check the directee's attitude toward possessions at every session.

The successful accomplishment of the three tasks of prayer, fasting, and almsgiving will result in a decentration from excessive concern for oneself and a supercentration of our whole life in God, God's Will, God's plan and destiny for us and the whole world. It will also result in at least an equal concern for the welfare and needs of our neighbor. If we wish to become totally Christ-like, then a Christ-like practice of the above three activities will result in an even greater concern for the welfare of others than for our own welfare. This willingness to sacrifice our welfare for the benefit of others is what Jesus means by the symbolism of the cross.

CHAPTER 8

How to Discern God's Will

One of the main tasks of a spiritual director is to help the directee discern God's Will. *Discernment* is a process of deciding and choosing the appropriate course of action in our relationship with God, with others, and toward ourselves. Religious discernment is an exercise of the gift of counsel by which the Holy Spirit enables us to see things from God's point of view. If we are willing to be open and receptive to the Holy Spirit, God will reveal his Will through our conscience as well as through special graces and insights. Discernment should be one of the main goals of our daily period of formal prayer. Through prayer we seek to make contact with God in order to discern his Will for us. If we are willing to spend some prime time each day in prayer and sincerely seek to know God's Will, we may confidently expect God to reveal his Will to us in one way or another.

One's life and destiny might be compared to a ball of twine that is portioned out to us a little bit at a time. The Holy Spirit reveals a few inches of our life's destiny each day. It is impossible for us to see ahead what is contained in our ball of twine. We have to be alert and open to the Holy Spirit in order to ascertain God's Will for us each day. We do this by prayer, silence, reflection, consultation with others, common sense, and experience. Each of us has a different ball of twine to unravel.

We mess up our own life as well as others when we try to use the ball of twine of someone else. Our particular destiny alone will bring us peace, contentment, fulfillment, and joy.

It is possible for sincere persons to make mistakes in discernment. Many fanatics and extremists appear to be quite sincere yet are often mistaken. Many of them base their decisions on the words of God in the Bible or on other sacred writings. The uncertainty regarding the accuracy of discernment is very disturbing for many people. They desperately seek for some sort of absolute certainty to reassure themselves and give them peace. However, if we wait for absolute certainty in our process of discernment, we would never be able to get out of bed in the morning, lest we slip and break our hip. All that God asks of us and all that is expected of us is that we do the best we can to arrive at the decision that will do the greatest good for both ourselves and others. Prayer and openness with an experienced spiritual director are two ways to discern God's Will in our regard.

Discernment is something that we do all day long. It goes into the many decisions we make regarding what we shall do or say, how to spend our time, when or what to eat, when to go to bed, when to get up, which TV program to watch, what book to read, how to react to the words and actions of others, and so on. Naturally, some of our decisions are more important than others, but all of our decisions have value and significance since they are based on the priorities we have chosen for our life and destiny. A serious, prayerful reflection on the gospel teachings of Jesus will oblige us to make a reversal of many of the priorities in our life. If we read the Gospels today as though we were reading them for the first time, we will find Jesus challenging us to reverse many of our priorities and goals of life.

Fifteen Ways to Discern God's Will

1. Use common sense to decide what will do the most good for everyone.
2. Use the three commandments of love of God, others, and self to discern which decision will fulfill our responsibilities to God, others, and self.
3. Make a list of all reasons for and against each possible option.
4. Take the problem to prayer and talk it over with God or Jesus.
5. Consult others whose judgment you trust.
6. Make a tentative decision, sleep on it for a few days, and then repeat the whole process of the previous five ways.
7. Try to imagine what Jesus might do if he were here in your place.
8. Try to find an appropriate scripture text that applies to your present situation, for example, a similar action in the public life of Jesus.
9. If the situation is quite serious, ask God for a sign.
10. If possible, experiment with a tentative decision and then check the immediate results of your action. "You will know them by their fruits" (Matt 7:16).
11. In case of doubt always retain the status quo. The burden of proof is always on the new direction that one is considering.
12. If both choices seem equally good, do the thing one least wants to do. We can presume that we are somewhat biased in our own favor.
13. Recognize the upper limits of one's endurance and keep a reserve of energy on which to rebuild one's strength.

14. Draw straws or toss a coin if none of the above methods indicate God's Will. This is what apostles did in choosing a successor to Judas.
15. As a last resort, if all else fails, open the Bible at random and try to find an answer to one's dilemma in the first text that meets the eye.

While here on Earth we will always live with uncertainty. Our trust in God's loving care must be sufficient to enable us to be at peace without absolute certitude. A good way to improve our ability to discern is to think back over our life and make a list of the decisions we made that were right and good and those that were mistakes. Study both lists to discover some clues as to why we were right and why we were wrong. This should be helpful when making decisions in the future. By discussing these decisions with a wise and experienced spiritual director, we usually are able to discern God's Will in our regard. Mistakes are inevitable. If we are honest enough to admit our errors, once we are made aware of them, no lasting harm will occur either to ourselves or others. We can accept the truth of Paul's words, "We know that all things work together for good for those who love God, who are called according to his purpose" (Rom 8:28).

Openness to the Holy Spirit

The primary purpose of spiritual direction is to help us maintain a constant openness to the Holy Spirit. The Holy Spirit is the presence of God's power, wisdom, and love within the world and within each of us. On the night before his death Jesus promised to send upon his apostles the gift of the Holy Spirit. He promised that this gift would remain with them always and they would never be left alone as orphans. This same Holy Spirit is available to us today and it is our responsibility to maintain a constant openness to the gifts of this Spirit.

We have many questions for which we seek an answer. We want to know what we are supposed to do with our life, what is our purpose on Earth? Why was I created? Where do I belong? Where do I fit into God's overall plan for his creation? Am I in the right place now? What is my destiny on Earth, my vocation? How can I best contribute to the welfare of the whole world? Where can I go to find the answers to these very basic questions regarding my life? The Holy Spirit will provide the answer to all of these questions. As the indwelling presence of God in the depths of our inner being, the Holy Spirit has been assigned the task of revealing to us God's Will and plan each day. In order to find the right answer to these basic questions of life, we need to maintain a ready openness to this indwelling Holy Spirit.

The Holy Spirit reveals God's Will to us primarily during our daily period of personal prayer. This is how Jesus was able to maintain a constant openness to the Holy Spirit during his public ministry. The Gospels tell us that Jesus would spend whole nights in prayer before making any important decision, for example, the choice of the twelve apostles. Even Jesus Christ had to take time out of his busy life in order to be alone with God and commune with the Holy Spirit. If Jesus Christ needed to spend hours each day in prayer, surely it is not expecting too much of us that we should try to arrange our busy schedule in order to give, if possible, a whole hour every day in order to communicate with God and open ourselves to the divine presence of God, the Holy Spirit.

Many Christians complain that they do not know how to pray. Many claim that their prayer period is a waste of time. If we really love God with our whole heart and soul, we will be willing to waste time with God each day. Actually if we make a sincere effort to pray, our prayer time is never wasted. St. Paul tells us that the Holy Spirit helps us in our present limitations. "Likewise the Spirit helps us in our weakness; for we do not know how to pray as we ought, but that very Spirit intercedes with sighs too deep for words. And God, who searches the heart, knows what is the mind of the Spirit, because the Spirit intercedes for the saints according to the will of God" (Rom 8:26–27). As the imminent presence of God in our inner being, the Holy Spirit will use the time we spend in prayer to work on our conscience and inspire us to find the right answer to all the questions which disturb us. Without our realizing it, the new insights we receive are gifts of the Holy Spirit.

One way to prepare ourselves for this openness to the Holy Spirit is to go through the Gospels and the New Testament and underline all the references to the love of God and the love of neighbor. Since the Holy Spirit is God's love, by reflecting on the biblical references to love we come to a better appreciation of what the Holy Spirit can do for us. As long as we sincerely try to maintain an open attitude to God and are ready and willing to go in any direction that God seems to be calling us, we will fulfill our God-appointed destiny. God is a great respecter of human freedom. He will never force his Will on us if we are unwilling to accept it. The main task of our daily prayer is to use whatever freedom we have to make a complete gift of ourselves to God. This is what Mary did at the Annunciation when she said, "Here am I, the servant of the Lord; let it be with me according to your word" (Luke 1:38).

Prayer time is the time when we say yes to God. There are many ways to say yes to God and thus open ourselves to the gifts of the Holy Spirit. In order to make this constant affirmative reply to God's call of grace, we need to trust God and convince ourselves that God is our friend. So our first task in prayer is to build up a complete confidence in God. God will never ask anything that will be harmful to us. God may ask us to make some sacrifices of things we hold near and dear. This will only happen when God, with his superior wisdom, knows that what he is asking of us is much better than what we are now enjoying. Sometimes our whole prayer period will be spent in efforts to build up our present shaky trust in God. We can do this by reflecting at length on God's promises, goodness, love, power, and wisdom.

Each time we pray we should make some sort of commitment of our whole life to God and to the doing of God's Will. One way to do this is to say to the Lord in prayer, "Anything, Lord, everything." By these words we give the Holy Spirit permission to do whatever God might wish to bestow on us. Thus we make a commitment to sacrifice our own selfish desires and to conform our life to all that God has planned for us.

In Luke's Gospel, Jesus tells us, "I came to bring fire to the earth, and how I wish it were already kindled" (Luke 12:49). This fire of God is the Holy Spirit or fire of God's love. A fire cannot burn unless it has fuel. Human hearts and souls and wills are the fuel on Earth that God needs in order for the fire of the Holy Spirit to become ignited. Thus, through us, the blaze of divine love will spring up all over the world. We are free to give over to God our life to be used as fuel for the fire of God's love. As long as we refuse to give ourselves over to the fire of the Holy Spirit, God is unable to establish the kingdom of love on Earth. Our daily prayer time is the proper moment to give God permission to use our life as fuel for his divine love.

The Holy Spirit is the invisible presence of God on Earth. The two biblical synonyms that best express the nature of the Holy Spirit are the *power of God* and the *love of God*. The Holy Spirit is the presence of the powerful love of God who is constantly at work in our lives, enabling us to know and to do God's Will, and to carry out our God-given purpose on Earth.

In the seventh chapter of John's Gospel, Jesus stands up and cries out, "Let anyone who is thirsty come to me, and let the one who believes in me drink. As the scripture has said, 'Out of the believer's heart shall flow rivers of living water.'" Now he said this about the Spirit, which believers in him were to receive; for as yet there was no Spirit, because Jesus was not yet glorified (John 7:37–39). In this scripture passage Jesus uses the image of water rather than fire to describe the power of the Holy Spirit in our lives. Water has the power to cleanse, to purify, to refresh, and to give life to the dry seed and dry sand. In a spiritual sense the Holy Spirit has been given the task of cleansing and purifying our soul of sin, of refreshing us with grace, and giving new life of grace. The Holy Spirit awakens the seeds of divine life that are present in the heart of each one of us. Without the Holy Spirit our life remains a dry, lifeless desert. Once the Holy Spirit pours over us the waters of divine grace, our whole life blossoms and fructifies. In this passage from John's Gospel, Jesus asserts that as a result of the presence of the Holy Spirit we also become rivers of living water that flow out on others and do for them what the Holy Spirit has already done for us. But first we thirst and desire these waters of the Holy Spirit. We use our freedom to go and drink from these waters of grace. Thus we open ourselves to the Holy Spirit each day in our prayer time and allow the power and love of God to fill our souls. Then we become rivers of living water for the whole world.

The Holy Spirit has an intense desire to become visibly present on Earth. Two thousand years ago the Second Person of the Holy Trinity became incarnate on Earth. Today we live in the age of the Holy Spirit and it is now the turn of the Third Person to become incarnate on Earth. This can only happen if we give ourselves over to the Holy Spirit in the same way that Mary did at the Annunciation. The Holy Spirit will never force itself on us, but waits patiently until we freely offer our heart and soul and body to be used by the Holy Spirit in the same way that God used the body that Mary gave to Jesus.

The Holy Spirit reveals God's Will to us in many different ways primarily through the words of the Bible. We speak of the Holy Spirit as the principal author who inspired the biblical writers to write what they did. The Holy Spirit also speaks to us through our common sense and through the voice of our conscience, through dreams, through a spiritual director or friend, through the various books we read, through experience, especially that of trial and error.

God reveals his Will to many people through their dreams. God uses dreams to reveal his Will more to some persons than to others. Through our dreams we make contact with the depths of our unconscious, which is much wiser than our conscious mind. Spiritual directors should use the literature of psychology on dream interpretation in order to help the directee discern God's message in the directee's dreams. I think Jung's method of dream interpretation is to be trusted rather than that of Freud. Two books to be recommended for working with dreams are those by Patricia Berne and Louis Savary, *Dreams and Spiritual Growth* and *Dream Symbol Work*. Also recommended is Jung's autobiography, *Memories, Dreams, Reflections*.

CHAPTER 9

Signs of Spiritual Progress

The Holy Spirit leads different souls in different ways. If a person follows his or her bliss (as Joseph Campbell calls it) and is well on the road to mature wholeness and holiness, one will discover that each person's journey of faith is unique and somewhat different from every other person. Spiritual directors must respect this uniqueness of each person who comes for direction. Nevertheless, there is need of some sort of measuring stick that the director can use in order to discern more clearly whether the directee is making substantial progress toward holiness and wholeness. In the Sermon on the Mount, Jesus gives us this test in his statement, "Thus you will know them by their fruits" (Matt 7:20). Regardless of the uniqueness of one's journey of faith, there are certain, telltale signs of spiritual progress present in the life of a healthy, growing, maturing person. These are the fruits of following the Will of God rather than one's own will.

One of the easiest ways to discern spiritual progress is a growing awareness of greater gratitude to God. Gratitude is a very positive way of practicing humility and counteracting pride and self-centeredness. It recognizes very clearly the meaning of Paul's challenge, "What do you have that you did not receive? And if you received it, why do you boast as if it were not a gift?" (1 Cor 4:7). Humility and gratitude are based on truth. When one acknowledges that everything is a gift from God, the best way to recognize this is to give humble thanks to God many times each day. Gratitude should be the very first thought upon awakening in the morning. We thank God for the gift of a new day of life and for the sleep and rest God has just given us. Gratitude should be the last thought at night before falling off to sleep. We thank God for the gifts of the whole day. As each hour of the day passes and a new experience of God's generosity is recognized, a quick look or word or thought of thanks may be lifted up to God. When someone compliments us for a job well done, we should accept the compliment graciously but at once pass the compliment on to God in an act of gratitude. As the years of our life pass by we should be able to discern a growing awareness of greater gratitude to God. If this be true, we have a clear sign that we are on the right road to holiness and that our journey of faith is progressing in the right direction.

A second sign of spiritual progress is a growing awareness of greater trust in God. More than any other teaching in the Gospels, Jesus insists on blind faith and trust in God. It is the key that unlocks the infinite treasures of God's love, mercy, and goodness. Confidence in God is emphasized more in the 150 Psalms of the Old Testament than any other aspect of our relationship with God. According to the Psalms this trust in God is based on two attributes of God's nature: his *Hesed,* his loving kindness, and his *Emath,* faithfulness to his Word and promises. God is absolutely dependable and trustworthy. This trust in God may be seen as based on these five qualities of God: his infinite power, goodness, wisdom, love, and truthfulness. As we continue to experience his goodness and reflect on these five divine traits, there should be a constant, growing awareness of greater trust in God.

A third sign of spiritual progress is a growing awareness of a greater intimacy with Jesus. This has been the experience of every Christian saint. The more real the mutual relationship of love between Jesus and a soul, the more holy that person is. An intimate relationship of love with Jesus is not developed overnight. Like any lasting relationship, it is something that one needs to work at for many years. The four Gospels of Matthew, Mark, Luke, and John need to be read and reread many times, constantly searching to probe the mystery of the "Word made flesh." Every detail of the Gospels will be studied, every word attributed to Jesus will be reflected on. Gradually, after many years, Jesus becomes alive as a real person, someone with whom one can relate in a deep, personal friendship; someone with whom one spends many hours in loving conversation. One begins to feel free to talk to Jesus about any detail of one's life. Gradually, either directly in the depths of one's inner being or through the words of Jesus in the Gospels, one will recognize the voice of Jesus speaking to oneself.

A fourth sign of spiritual progress is a growing awareness of humble submission of our human will to the Will of God. As we grow in holiness there is less resistance to the carrying out of God's Will. We begin to recognize that God knows what is best and that it is the height of foolishness to pit our knowledge and wisdom against that of God. God has our best interests at heart and we benefit when we submit our will to his Will. Therefore, there is now less and less time between the moment we become aware of what God wills for us and the moment we begin to carry out God's Will.

A fifth sign of spiritual growth is the adoption of a simplicity of lifestyle. As we progress in holiness our desires for worldly goods and sensual pleasures become less and less. We become content to do with less of the good things of Earth rather than more and more. It is not that we do not appreciate the value of God's earthly gifts; if anything, our appreciation grows. Even the simplest bodily and earthly pleasures take on a mystical, spiritual value. We no longer need an overabundance of earthly possessions and pleasures in order to satisfy us. Now our love and concern for others is so great that we are more ready to share with them the many gifts of God. As St. Paul says, "It is a question of a fair balance between your present abundance and their need, so that their abundance may be for your need, in order that there may be a fair balance" (2 Cor 8:13–14).

A sixth sign of spiritual progress is an ever greater desire and longing for God, for God's love, and for holiness. This desire becomes so intense that it dominates all other desires. The motivation behind this desire is a more and more pure love of God and a less and less love of ourselves apart from God. We want to be holy because this is what God wants for us rather than what we might want for ourselves. This longing for God, which we begin to experience, explains why so many of the saints looked forward to death rather than being afraid of death.

A seventh sign of spiritual growth is the fact that the thought of God more and more predominates one's attention. This thought of God is more consistently present throughout the waking hours of the day than was true at an earlier period of one's life. One's conscious mind and will are more centered in God and the things of God than was true in the past. This is a very authentic sign that our love for God is growing. When we are deeply in love with another person, it is almost impossible to get the thought of that person out of our mind. Thinking about the beloved is one way of staying in the presence of that person. It is the way we are able to send out a constant stream of love and desire toward the object of our love.

An eighth sign of spiritual progress is an ever-greater experience of deep, inner peace regardless of the outer circumstances of our life. This is a threefold peace: peace with God, with others, and with our inner self. St. Augustine defines *peace* as the tranquility of order. First, the right order of our life is that God and God's Will must always come first. Second, we will try to love others the way Jesus loved his disciples. Third, we will show the proper respect, honor, and love for the divine gift of our self. When these different loves are in the proper order, we will be at peace. As we grow spiritually, we succeed in putting the proper order into our lives and the result of this will be an ever-growing experience of deep, inner peace.

A ninth sign of spiritual growth is a more positive attitude toward everything. As we grow spiritually, we are able to overcome our negativity and begin to adopt a very positive, loving attitude toward ourselves, God, others, the world, and the future. This in turn enables us to be much more patient with ourselves, with others, and with God. We become more tolerant of others, more gentle and forgiving, more willing to live and let live, more tolerant of differences without becoming disturbed. Others will recognize that we are less rigid, less harsh, and less judgmental. We will be able to find something good to say about everyone and every situation.

A tenth sign of spiritual progress is greater self-control. We are able to control our anger, our temper. We are no longer so quick to lose our patience and temper as in the past. We are no longer at the mercy of those sudden urges to eat, drink, and indulge ourselves in one way or another. We have now learned to think before we speak and so do not find ourselves saying things we deeply regret afterward. All of our inner drives, including our sexual drives, become more and more subject to the control of our conscious will, which in turn becomes more and more submissive to the Will of God.

An eleventh sign of spiritual growth is a greater generosity in sharing with others. This sharing includes not only money and possessions, but also our talents, time, energy, experience, and spiritual gifts. As we grow spiritually, we become aware that everything we have belongs to God. We are merely God's stewards and one day will have to render a strict account of what use we made of all the things we now call our own.

"What shall I return to the Lord for all his bounty to me?" (Ps 116:12). One of the best ways to make such a return is by sharing with others the many treasures and gifts that God has so generously endowed us.

A twelfth sign of spiritual progress is a greater willingness to change our old ways of thinking, acting, judging, and speaking. We never get too old to learn. We are expected to grow in wisdom, knowledge, love, and grace throughout our life on Earth. An authentic sign of such growth is the willingness to change old ways and adopt new ways. If we become too set in our old habits and ways of thinking, we stop progressing both in psychological maturity and spiritual holiness. We should always be interested in learning something new. We never have the last word about any truth. If we close our minds to new truth and become rigid and set in our accustomed ways of thinking and acting, we actually begin to regress to an earlier, more infantile way of life.

Fruits of the Holy Spirit

Following the Latin Vulgate translation of the Bible by St. Jerome, the Church has traditionally spoken of twelve fruits of the Holy Spirit. Actually, scripture scholars agree that the original text of Galatians gives only nine fruits. It would seem that Jerome simply expanded three of these fruits by using two words instead of just one to express the full meaning of these fruits. The New Revised Standard Version lists these fruits as follows: love, joy, peace, patience, kindness, goodness, faithfulness, gentleness, and self-control (Gal 5:22–23). In order to appreciate the full meaning of these nine terms, I would like to suggest the following terms to expand the original words. Besides patience, we might think of this fruit as including also forbearance, long-suffering, and the willingness to bear wrongs patiently. We could expand the word *goodness* to include also generosity. The word *faithfulness* should also include faith, that quality which Jesus claimed, "If you had faith the size of a mustard seed, you could say to this mulberry tree, 'Be uprooted and planted in the sea,' and it would obey you" (Luke 17:6). *Gentleness* should be expanded to include tolerance and moderation. Finally, *self-control* may be expanded to include balance, purity, chastity, and continence.

Most of these fruits of the Holy Spirit will be found in the twelve signs of spiritual progress that have already been listed. Further reflection on the various terms used to describe the fruits of the Holy Spirit will give us additional ways to discern whether we are indeed growing in holiness and wholeness on our journey of faith. Our Lord clearly states that we will be known by our fruits, "You will know them by their fruits. Are grapes gathered from thorns, or figs from thistles? In the same way, every good tree bears good fruit, but the bad tree bears bad fruit. A good tree cannot bear bad fruit, nor can a bad tree bear good fruit. Every tree that does not bear good fruit is cut down and thrown into the fire. Thus you will know them by their fruits" (Matt 7:16–20).

It is not necessary that one discern progress in all of the twelve signs or twelve fruits of the Holy Spirit. If one can see progress in even one or two of them, this is a clear sign that some progress is being made on the path to holiness. The more signs where progress can be clearly discerned, the swifter is our progress toward our goal of holiness and spiritual maturity. On the other hand, if in one or more of these signs of progress or fruits of the Spirit there is clear evidence of regression or going in the opposite direction, these are the areas that should be addressed by the spiritual director and directee.

There is an interconnection between these signs of progress and fruits of the Spirit. Any substantial progress in any one of them will make it easier to progress in the others. One should not become discouraged at the apparent lack of progress in some of these fruits. There is a proper time in the course of our life when we need to work, first, on one and then on another of the signs and fruits. It is the task of the spiritual director to help the directee discern which fruit or which sign of progress that God is calling this person to try to emphasize at this particular point of one's journey of faith. Also, in attempting to discern spiritual progress, the directee and director should compare one's present situation with that of a year ago or even two, three, or five years ago. Spiritual progress is usually slow and indiscernible from day to day or month to month. Over the years of one's life, there should be growth in all the fruits of the Holy Spirit and in all twelve signs of spiritual progress.

Little Way of Spiritual Childhood

During her short life of twenty-four years, St. Thérèse of Lisieux developed a method for measuring one's spiritual progress. She called it "The Little Way of Spiritual Childhood." She tells us that she gradually developed this Little Way during the nine years of religious life before her death. She called her teaching the Little Way to emphasize its adaptability for use by average people. Traditionally sanctity has been considered as possible only for great and heroic souls who performed miracles and other remarkable spiritual feats. St. Thérèse insists that none of these are necessary to reach sanctity. This does not mean that sanctity is easy and that tepid, selfish, or careless souls are automatically assured of perfection. Rather holiness can be found in doing the most simple and ordinary tasks with extraordinary love and confidence in God. Child-like is the opposite of being childish. *Littleness* refers to one's attitude toward oneself. One recognizes one's helplessness apart from God. Pride is the greatest obstacle to holiness because it is a dishonest and false attribution of good to self and thus a stealing of credit from God, the source of all goodness. The Little Way makes humility the foundation for the whole structure of sanctity because humility is truth and authenticity. "To remain little means to recognize one's nothingness, to expect everything from God, and not to worry too much about one's faults."

As a consequence of this recognition of one's littleness, a necessary dependence on God's providence will grow. Thus, an unlimited confidence in God is another characteristic mark of spiritual childhood. "God proportions His goodness to accord with the degree of our confidence in Him and takes great delight in showering His greatest favors upon the most weak and helpless, provided that we trust ourselves completely to Him and have good will" (*Letters to the Missions*, chap. 11, p. 155). Thérèse assures us that "never can we have too much confidence in the good God....We obtain from the good God quite as much as we hope for." She based her confidence not only on God's goodness and mercy and love, but also in a special way on God's justice. "It is because He is just that the good God is compassionate and full of gentleness, slow to punish and abounding in mercy. He knows our frailty. He remembers that we are but dust. He takes into account our weakness. What then need I fear?"

Along with humility and a bold confidence in God, Thérèse insists that her Little Way includes having immense desires of holiness.

I have the daring confidence that one day I shall become a great saint. I am not trusting on my own merits, for I have none; but I trust in Him who is virtue and holiness itself....Our dreams and desires for perfection are not fancies, since Jesus himself has commanded us to realize them, saying, "Be you perfect as your heavenly Father is perfect."...Little children have a right to be daring with their parents....Children do not reflect on the import of their words. Nevertheless, if their parents are possessed of immense treasures, they do not hesitate about gratifying all the desires of the little ones whom they cherish more than themselves. (Chap. 4, p. 49)

Experiencing these immense desires, Thérèse tells us that they became a veritable martyrdom until she found chapters 12 and 13 of first Epistle to Corinthians.

I read that all cannot be apostles, prophets, doctors, etc. Without becoming discouraged I continued my reading and this sentence consoled me: "Yet strive after the better gifts and I will point out to you a yet more excellent way." Then the Apostle explains how all the most perfect gifts are nothing without love, that charity is the way that leads most surely to God. I finally had rest....Charity gave me the key to my vocation. I understood that if the Church had a body composed of different members, the most necessary and most noble of all could not be lacking to it (namely a heart). So I understood that it was love alone that made the Church's members act....I understood that love comprised all vocations. Then in the excess of my joy, I cried out, my vocation is love! (Chapter 11, pp. 154–55)

Love is the clearest of all signs of spiritual progress.

In times past, victims pure and spotless were the only ones accepted by God. To satisfy divine justice perfect victims were necessary, but the law of love has succeeded the law of fear. Love has chosen me as a holocaust, me a weak and imperfect creature....In order that love be fully satisfied, it is necessary that it lower itself to nothingness and then transform this nothingness into fire....I am the smallest of creatures, I know my misery and my feebleness, but I know also how much noble and generous hearts love to do good. I beg you then, O blessed inhabitants of heaven, I beg you to adopt me as your child. To you alone will be the glory which you will make me merit, but deign to answer my prayer. I dare to ask you to obtain for me your twofold spirit. O my Jesus, I love you. I love the Church, my mother. I recall that "the smallest act of pure love is of more value to her than all other works together." I beg you to cast your divine glance upon a great number of little souls. I beg you to choose a legion of little victims worthy of your love. (Chapter 11, pp. 155–59)

CHAPTER 10

Direction for Different Levels of Faith

Faith is a fundamental experience that cannot be reduced to anything else. It is the word we use to describe our relationship with God or whatever it is that we judge to have absolute value and power. There are different ways of relating to God (i.e., different levels of faith). In any large group of Christians, we will find persons at each of these levels. There is a different way to direct and guide persons at the different levels. There are different methods of prayer that are best suited for each of these levels of faith.

Writers from the very beginning of Christianity have attempted to describe and give names to the different levels of faith. St. Paul speaks of two levels of faith: infancy and adulthood. Later writers of Apostolic Times speak of beginners and proficients in the faith. By the fourth century, Evagrius Ponticus is able to distinguish three different levels of faith. The Pseudo-Dionysius in the sixth century gave names to these three levels that became traditional for many centuries: Purgative, Illuminative, and Unitive Ways. The Purgative Way was the way of beginners and consisted primarily of purging one's life of sin and evil. The Illuminative Way was for proficients in the faith who were concerned in illuminating their souls with the Christian virtues. Those souls who have attained a deep and constant union with God belong to the Unitive Way. In the sixteenth century St. Teresa of Avila, in her book *Interior Castle,* further divided the levels of faith into what she called the seven mansions. The first two mansions would belong to the Purgative Way, third and fourth mansions would be the Illuminative Way, and three highest mansions would comprise the Unitive Way.

At the beginning of the twentieth century, Abbe Saudreau, in his book *The Degrees of the Spiritual Life,* gave names to these seven stages or levels of faith: Believing Souls, Good Christian Souls, Devout Souls, Fervent Souls, Perfect Souls, Heroic Souls, and Great Saints. Saudreau along with many other spiritual writers such as Reginald Garrigou-Lagrange, have attempted to describe the different methods of spiritual direction and prayer that were appropriate to each of these seven levels of faith. In recent years many writers have used the insights of depth psychology to give a clearer description of the different stages of faith and maturity. Among the more well known of these writers are Abraham Maslow, Lawrence Kohlberg, Erik Erikson, James Fowler, and Evelyn and James Whitehead. My book *Arise: A Christian Psychology of Love* devotes chapter 4 to describe the stages of growth that frequently occur at seven-year intervals. A good description of the seven levels of faith is found in the *Hall-Tonna Inventory of Values,* published by Paulist Press. Using a criterion of 125 basic human values, Dr. Brian Hall and Rev. Benjamin Tonna have developed an instrument to determine in which of seven levels or cycles of faith development a person is presently living. In addition, they offer valuable suggestions for the spiritual direction and psychological counseling of persons at each of these seven levels. In this present chapter we will attempt to use the insights of all these writers to make suggestions for the spiritual direction of persons at the seven different levels of faith. Since direction differs for each of the faith levels, we will briefly describe each level in order to help identify who might belong to that level and then offer suggestions for the spiritual direction of each level.

First Level of Faith

This first level is the faith of very small children as well as desperate people who are fighting for survival and are on the verge of losing everything. It is the level of persons who feel totally helpless to protect themselves from some almighty power that threatens their very existence. The world is seen as an alien and mysterious place ruled by a distant authority over which they have no control. Survival and physical security are their exclusive interests and this results in a very limited view of everything beyond immediate personal needs. Persons at this level usually have a very negative attitude toward the world since they see it as filled with constant threats to their survival. This is the worldview of deeply oppressed and destitute people. If the environment is threatening enough, everyone begins to react out of this worldview. Even Jesus Christ on the cross experienced something similar to this level of faith when he cried out, "My God, my God, why have you forsaken me?" (Matt 27:46). God is seen as a distant savior who rules the world in some mysterious, awesome way. Drug addicts, alcoholics, and street people who still cling to belief in God will usually be found at this first level of faith. Perhaps as many as 50 percent of the people of the world, especially those who live in the underdeveloped countries of Latin America and Africa, are at this level.

The primary objective of spiritual direction for people at this level is to do all in one's power to relieve them or help them relieve themselves of the evils that presently threaten their security. The leaders of the Catholic Church in Brazil give us a marvelous example of the proper way to direct and help people at this first level that Hall-Tonna calls the Primal Cycle, Kohlberg calls it the Pre-Conventional Level of Development, Erikson calls it Basic Trust versus Mistrust. The amazing thing is that in Brazil, Dom Helder Camara and other church leaders through the movement called Basic Christian Communities have been able to help these destitute people attain a much higher and more satisfying level of life.

A second objective in helping people at this first level is to give them hope by helping them to see God as a truly loving parent who will surely one day see that justice is done for them. Admittedly this is extremely difficult for persons who are totally destitute. Without a strong belief in life after death, it is usually impossible for persons at this level to hold on to a blind trust in God. The story of the rich man and the beggar Lazarus in the sixteenth chapter of Luke is one of the gospel stories that have enabled the Basic Christian Communities of Brazil and other Latin American countries to build up their trust in God. It is the gospel paradox so frequently used by Jesus to convince the First Level people of his time that God is ultimately trustworthy and in his own mysterious way and time will take care of them.

For many people at this first level, their image of God is filled with magic, superstition, and taboos. A taboo is a dangerous, supernatural power that one has no control over but needs to be placated by superstitious, magical words, signs, and actions. Theirs is a very simplistic faith with a limited view of everything beyond their own need of survival. In such a situation people become dependent on anyone who can give them security and thus become the pawns of autocratic, absolute dictators. There are many examples of unscrupulous leaders who have taken advantage of such desperate people to attain and maintain power. A good leader will come down to the level of these desperate people and find ways to help them survive and achieve a greater security.

The prayer form proper to persons at this first level of faith is almost exclusively vocal prayers that are desperate cries for help. They are the cries of a person confronted by overwhelming odds but who still believes and hopes in God. It is interesting to note that a great many of the Psalms in the Bible are just such desperate cries for help. Examples of such Psalms are: 6, 10, 13, 17, 22, 35, 38, 39, 69, 74, 83, 86, 88, 102, 140, and 142. In addition many other passages of the Old Testament, especially Jeremiah and some of the other prophets, are clear examples of the type of prayer appropriate to persons at this first level of faith. This would indicate that many of the people with whom Yahweh had to deal throughout the history of Israel were persons at this primal level.

Few persons at this first level of faith will come to us seeking spiritual direction. Their needs are considerably more basic than the luxury of spiritual direction. If we are to give spiritual direction to these desperate people, we will have to go out looking for them. In comparison with the undeveloped countries of the world, we will not find as many persons in our country at this level. Nevertheless, they are around if we will go looking for them. Besides the obvious drug addicts, desperate alcoholics, and other destitute people, the victims of AIDS as well as people with terminal illnesses may well be at this first level of faith. Almost all of us will revert back to this primal level if we find ourselves in a sufficiently desperate situation. In many ways the persons at this first level are the people most in need of spiritual direction. Therefore, if we want to take seriously this ministry of spiritual direction we will make the effort to search out and help people at this level.

Second Level of Faith

The second level of faith is the level of faith proper to grade-school children. It is the second stage of the Purgative Way, the Second Mansion of St. Teresa of Avila, the Familial Cycle of the Hall-Tonna Inventory of Values, Mythic-Literal Faith of James Fowler, stage two of Kohlberg's Pre-Conventional level. Erikson calls it the Industry versus Inferiority stage. Saudreau calls persons at this level Good Christians. Probably 30 to 50 percent of the Catholics who regularly attend Mass in this country are at this second level. In some other countries, especially where the faith is persecuted or people are uneducated, the percentage of Catholics and other Christians at this level may be as high as 80 percent. This is the level of faith of most Christians who are illiterate or poorly educated in religion. This is the level of faith of almost all fundamentalists, both Catholic and Protestant. It is the level of faith to which most modern-day televangelists appeal. It was the level of faith of the Pharisees and most of the people to whom Jesus preached.

The principle of reciprocity governs the divine-human relationship for persons at this level. The relationship with God becomes a business deal, a tit-for-tat. If I do this for God, then I can expect God to do that for me. One's religion becomes a system of rewards and punishments directly proportionate to one's good or bad actions. It is the righteousness of good works against which St. Paul so strongly argues in his Epistles to the Romans and Galatians. Sorrow for sin at this level of faith will be what is called *imperfect contrition*—sorrow because one dreads the loss of heaven and the pains of hell. The prayer of persons at this level will almost exclusively be prayers of petition that amount to an attempt to bargain with God. It is a simplistic, nonreflective, uncomplicated faith with a very human image of God as a "Big Daddy" up in the sky or perhaps a "Bogeyman" who can just as easily condemn one to hell. Usually, persons at this level have an excessive fear of mortal sin and the loss of eternal salvation.

Persons at this level have a great dependence on the group or institution to which they belong, since they feel very insecure when alone. They feel incapable of making their own decisions and so usually give blind, unquestioning obedience to the leaders of the group. Also, there is usually an insistence on a rigid application of the rules and laws of the group to which they belong, a conservative clinging to past traditions and a great resistance to change. There is little spontaneity in their prayer forms; instead there is an exclusive dependence on the prayer forms composed by the church authorities. Usually there is a very negative attitude toward the outside world that is seen as hostile, alien, and a constant threat to their well-being. This is often the faith of people who are persecuted for their religious belief. So true is this that in time of persecution even those at some higher level of faith will often revert back to this second level. It is the faith of persons under attack for their belief in God who feel the need to pull in the flanks and circle the wagons to obtain mutual protection and support. At such a time they feel the need of a strong authority to tell them what to do, otherwise they may go to pieces.

The faith of the second level is one dimensional and simplistic with an insistence on the literal, fundamentalist interpretation of the words of the Bible and the laws and decisions of religious authorities. Persons at this level seem incapable of dealing with gray areas but insist that everything be either black or white, right or wrong. They want simplistic answers to all religious questions since, like small children, they are unable to deal with complex issues. Thus they show a great dependence on the decisions of their leaders and invest these leaders with divine, superhuman authority. "Father knows best"—A proud, unscrupulous leader can do great harm by taking unfair advantage of the blind obedience of followers who are stuck at this second level of faith. "Do it because I say so"—The leader becomes responsible for all-important decisions with little or no consideration for the opinion or input of the followers. This is necessary when dealing with small children or illiterate masses but is a disaster when the followers are competent to make their own decisions.

Persons at the second level have a great nostalgia for the old Latin, Tridentine Mass, the old religious practices of the pre-Vatican II Church. The traditional forms of prayer and devotions learned in childhood are preferred over new methods of prayer or revised, updated liturgies. There is a great dependence on the externals of religion such as medals, scapulars, relics, and so forth. They feel the need to touch and have physical contact with some earthly manifestation of God. They love to be present when there is exposition of the Blessed Sacrament and be a part of the perpetual adoration of Eucharist. They flock on pilgrimages to shrines where God or the Blessed Mother have manifested themselves in some way.

Persons at this level usually have a low, poor self-image and are full of fear of sin, hell, pain, death, and the world. They have an excessive fear of failure and high state of anxiety. Their religion is based primarily on fear of God rather than love of God. This second level is the faith proper for children at the grade-school level. Ideally, the adolescent Christian should be able to graduate from second to third level of faith. Many adults never advance beyond the second level or revert back to this level as a safe haven in times of crisis. An equally unfortunate situation exists when church leaders insist on treating all their followers as though they were stuck in this second level of faith. A real problem for leaders exists when a portion of their flock is at the second level while others are at a higher level. The challenge for leaders and spiritual directors is to find a way to guide people at this second level through the third, adolescent level of faith to the levels of faith appropriate for mature, adult Christians. This will be accomplished primarily by an ongoing, adult, religious education program.

The first task of a spiritual director is to help persons at this level to overcome false images of God and to gain a true knowledge of a God who loves them very dearly. Thus they can be led from a servile fear of God to the love of God, from imperfect contrition to perfect contrition, from insecurity to security, from a low self-image to an appreciation of their value as a child of God. Instead of a blind, childish obedience to the decisions of their superiors, they need to be given sufficient knowledge of God and religion that will enable them to trust their own conscience and good judgment in making moral decisions.

Much of the spiritual direction of persons at this level will consist of gradually leading them from the Purgative Way to the Illuminative Way. Persons at the second level seldom make a deliberate decision to commit a mortal sin, a deliberate decision to cut themselves off from God. However, their love of God is not sufficient to cause them to avoid all deliberate, venial sin. If they are ever to graduate from the second level of faith, they will need to reach a sufficient love of God that they would rather die than deliberately offend God even in a small way. In order to encourage them to take this new step in their love of God, it will help to appeal to their enlightened self-interest by explaining all the advantages to themselves that result from the practice of the love of God. This was the method that Jesus used in the Gospel when speaking to persons at this second level.

Persons at the second level will frequently seek spiritual direction either after some deep, faith experience of God or because of some serious faith problem, difficulty, or temptation. Spiritual directors need to realize that it is impossible for a person to move from one level of faith to a higher level without a faith experience of God's presence, power, and love. These moments of grace occur every day in the life of the average person. Most people, however, fail to recognize them. As a result the grace comes and goes without making any change in the life of the directee. The spiritual director has the task of recognizing them in the life of the directee and making the person aware of them. The director plays the part of spiritual catalyst that brings together the necessary elements of a faith experience. In addition, the director has the task of instructing the directee in the proper response of love to make to each moment of grace. Because of fear and anxiety in the directee, much of the spiritual direction for persons at the second level will consist of encouragement after a fall or failure to live up to their good resolutions. A Cursillo Weekend or other weekend retreats are some of the best tools to give the needed courage to a person stuck in the second level to break away from their old habits of faith and attempt new ways of relating to God. A daily period of prayer and frequent fasting or other form of self-discipline will obtain for them the needed grace to put God first in their lives above all worldly attractions.

Third Level of Faith

The third level of faith is the faith proper to the adolescent teenager, however, many Catholics and other Christians cling to this level of faith all of their adult life. This is especially tragic when the religious leaders insist on remaining at this level of faith since they are then unable to understand the needs and problems of those members of the church who have graduated to one of the higher levels. Yet it would appear that at the present time a large number of our religious leaders are indeed stuck at this third level. There is a tendency for leaders at the third level to imagine that all of their followers are back at the second level and treat them accordingly. When this occurs, Christians at the fourth or fifth levels of faith lose confidence in their leaders.

The third level is called the Institutional Cycle by Hall-Tonna, Synthetic-Conventional faith by James Fowler, Interpersonal-Normative morality by Kohlberg, and Identity versus Identity Diffusion by Erickson. Saudreau calls those at this level Devout Christians. It is the first stage of the Illuminative Way and thus marks a shift from a negative to a more positive worldview. However, persons at the third level still see the world as an alien, hostile danger with which they are unable to cope and so seek the support of a group of like-minded persons. The typical teenager sees the need to cut oneself off from the parents in order to exercise one's newfound freedom. However, feeling unable to stand alone, the adolescent usually turns for support to a peer group. This peer group of like-minded persons is seen as a necessary protection against a hostile environment that surrounds one on every side. Persons at this level show great loyalty to the particular group or institution that they have personally chosen to join. Why not remain loyal to the family group? The adolescent was not free to choose the family to which one belongs, and personal freedom of choice becomes a necessity if one is ever to become an adult.

The third level of faith may be seen as a necessary novitiate for every human being on the journey of faith. Those at the second level are simply unable to go immediately from their simple, child-like faith to the fully mature faith of adults. They need ten or fifteen intermediate years at the third level to prepare them gradually for the adult faith of the fourth level. During these novitiate years, with the support of their peer group, they are expected to bring to maturity their human faculties. These would include intellect, will, imagination, feelings, senses, memory, intuition, and so on.

What are some of the reasons why many persons become stuck at the third level and never succeed in moving on to the higher levels of adult faith? The primary reason is a deep fear and distrust of themselves, a deep inner insecurity in the presence of a hostile, worldly environment. God is seen as a deep, inaccessible mystery whom one is unable or unwilling to encounter alone. Many people exaggerate the dangers to their salvation and minimize their ability to cope with these evil forces. They are afraid to take the faith stance of the fourth level that requires one to trust one's own conscience and power to make the right decision. Instead, they find their security in the institutional church or the support of their peer group. The less one is willing to trust one's own judgment and ability to make decisions in matters of faith and morals, the more one is willing to rely on the church or peer group to make such decisions. The church, the state, or other primal group to which one has pledged loyalty is given blind obedience and is endowed with divine, infallible authority. A tragic example of such blind obedience was the behavior of the majority of the German people in regard to Hitler during the Nazi era.

The unwillingness to assume an adult responsibility for one's own decisions frequently results from a lack of good experiences of love. If one has never had a first-hand experience of receiving a mature love from others, one is usually unwilling to assume the personal risk that is involved in making the decision to love God with a mature, adult love. In order to move beyond the third level of faith one must have the courage to make a total commitment to God as a significant other who becomes one's inseparable companion, guide, and support. Such a relationship of love with God requires the willingness to stand alone before God and be totally responsible for one's life and decisions. When one is unable or unwilling to make such a faith commitment, one tries to find security in the group—"In numbers there is strength." The result is a form of institutional narcissism where blind, unquestioning loyalty is given to the group or institution. Such an institutional triumphalism usually results in the neglect of personal rights and the raising of the institution to a divine level.

How does one break away from the tyranny of the group and find the courage to make an adult, mature commitment of faith in God? Good, spiritual direction or guidance by a trusted, mature adult Christian is almost a necessity to escape the enslavement of the third level. In addition, a resolute will, an intense desire to become mature and independent, and much perseverance are required. Also, good faith experiences of God's presence, God's love, and God's power at work in one's life are essential. One of the best ways for this to occur is through good, group liturgies where a mature, faith-filled group together experiences the presence of God. The Cursillo movement, especially at the high-school level (Christian Awakening) and college level (College Encounter) is one of the best tools for good faith experiences. Many good experiences of intimacy with Jesus Christ will occur if one is willing to spend an hour each day making a personal application of the Gospels to one's life situation. All of the recommendations concerning spiritual direction in this book are applicable to persons at this level since this is first time in one's life that such guidance is fully effective.

Fourth Level of Faith

This is the level of a mature, adult Christian. Ideally, one might hope to attain this fourth level sometime between the ages of twenty-one and twenty-eight. For the average person as much as thirty years will be required to fulfill all the tasks of this level. An ideal age to finish the fourth level and graduate to the fifth level of faith would be fifty-six. See chapter 4 of *Arise: A Christian Psychology of Love* for a further explanation of the reasons for choosing these numbers. Of course every person is unique and will need to discern the particular timetable appropriate to each one's destiny.

Brian Hall calls this level the Interpersonal Cycle to distinguish it from the previous Institutional Cycle. James Fowler calls this stage Individuative-Reflective Faith. For Erikson it is the Intimacy versus Self-Absorption stage, while Kohlberg calls it Law and Order Morality. It is the second stage of the

Illuminative Way and Saudreau calls those in this level the Fervent Christians. It is the time when the individual breaks away from the tyranny of the group and is ready and willing to trust the voice of the inner self, willing to stand alone apart from the crowd. One is willing to risk going one's own personal, individual way even when it is at cross-purposes to the group, institution, church, family, society, and state to which one belongs.

The prospect of breaking away from the group and launching out on one's own usually brings on a serious identity crisis. At such a crisis one needs to find a whole new center for one's life, a center within one's self—"To thy own self be true." A whole new way of life will have to be worked out once the decision of adult faith is made. One needs to go back over all the previously held faith assumptions and make a new decision of faith in regard to each one of them. After looking at all the options available, one is willing to take a new stand, personally chosen, relying primarily on one's own conscience. This is called the *demythologizing* of one's faith and the choosing of a new myth to symbolize one's adult faith choice. Naturally, such a task is fraught with dangers of going off the deep end and making a mess of one's life. For this reason, spiritual direction by a mature, well-balanced, wise director is almost a necessity for a person at the fourth level. More than any other level of faith a person at this adult juncture needs the help of a good spiritual guide. Without such a guide most people will go astray. If such guidance is not available, many persons at this level will revert back to level two or three and find security the rest of their life in the group or institution to which they belong.

People at this level usually have a hidden agenda when they go to God in prayer. Externally, they may mouth a total commitment to God, but secretly and unconsciously they still want their own way. We don't suddenly break away from our old faith in the group and strike out alone on the journey of faith. A good spiritual director will show great patience and tolerance for a person at this level of faith. Slowly but surely the directee will be made aware of his or her hidden agendas of selfishness and gradually be led to a more and more perfect gift of self to God.

God usually leads a person into this fourth level by giving one a new awareness of the value of personal dignity and an appreciation of one's unique place in God's love and plan. The first demythologizing occurs when one is able to step back and see the groups and institutions to which one belongs from a more objective viewpoint. One can appreciate their value but they are no longer seen as purely divine but rather as a very human invention to help us on our journey of faith. No longer is one willing to give blind obedience to another human being but only to God. This commitment of one's life to God must ultimately be determined by one's own conscience rather than allowing some group to make such a decision.

The prayer life of a person at this level will undergo many changes from one's former methods of prayer. This change often begins with a deep dislike and dissatisfaction with all structured forms of prayer. This usually leads to a rejection of older, formal methods of prayer such as the rosary, the office, and so on. One prefers spontaneous, personalized prayer with great freedom of choice in prayer. The task of the spiritual director is to encourage this openness to new ways of prayer. Otherwise, a person at this level may imagine that he or she is actually losing faith in God and prayer. A person at this level should be encouraged to make many spontaneous contacts with God throughout the day and night, practicing a continual remembrance of God's presence in our life. One good way to accomplish this is through the practice of *centering prayer*. A great openness to the Holy Spirit is needed at this time in order to discover how God wishes to relate to a person at this level. Also, the five methods of prayer explained in the book *Prayer and Temperament* are recommended for persons at the fourth level. A person at this level will still be primarily concerned with one's own needs and the needs of loved ones. A spiritual director will gradually lead a person at this level to a more global consciousness.

A person at the fourth level needs a strong, dependable support system that understands the crises and experiences of this level and can give mature, balanced guidance and thus assist a person through the identity crisis and the journey of faith toward the higher levels. A spiritual director will be able to give some of this support but should help a person find a new support group to replace the reliance on the old peer groups on which one depended at the third level. This new support group should consist of persons at the fourth or higher levels of faith who can mutually encourage one another to be faithful to God's calls of grace.

Fifth Level of Faith

The fifth level is what Hall-Tonna calls the Collaborative Cycle because it is the beginning of a global consciousness that enlists the collaboration of everyone of good will. James Fowler calls it Conjunctive Faith, Kohlberg calls it Post-Conventional Autonomy, and Erikson calls it Generativity versus Stagnation. Saudreau speaks of those at this level as Perfect Souls or Contemplative Souls because this is the first stage of the Unitive Way and therefore the beginning of Passive Contemplation. Ricour speaks of this level as the Second Naiveté because this is where a person discovers the new symbols and myths that will best express the new relationship with God attained at this time. These new symbols help one to understand and maintain a deeper unity with God and the transcendental values connected with God. Some of these values are justice, love, unity, beauty, and goodness.

An integration of one's whole life and outlook on reality occurs at this level. Much that was necessarily repressed and ignored at the fourth level can now be incorporated into one's life. Previously it was necessary to carve out and establish one's own special niche and place in the world. Now a new global consciousness occupies one's attention. There is a willingness to assume not only the responsibility for one's own life but also to do all in one's power to save the whole world. Realizing that a rugged individual cannot alone cope with all the problems of the world, one is now ready to work together with others as a team to resolve these problems. One is now willing to consider the needs of others as of equal importance to one's own needs.

A characteristic of persons at the fifth level is balance. One is able to integrate opposing values into a new unity without exaggerating or neglecting either side. Nothing worthwhile is neglected but a place is found for everything and everyone. Two other characteristics emerge at this level as a result of balance and integration. First of all, a new creativity is seen in a person at this level, whereby one is able to use every possible circumstance or situation in life to build up the kingdom of God on Earth. Persons at this level become co-creators with God in constructing a new creation. Second, a great simplicity of lifestyle is evident in one's whole life. Nothing is wasted or misused, but a useful place is found for everyone and everything.

The fifth level of faith is a time for much self-criticism and a purification of one's motives. One is now able to see the whole of one's life with great objectivity, noting both the good as well as the bad. One's unconscious shadow becomes daily more open for observation. There is a peaceful and even joyful acceptance of one's limitations as well as strengths. This is a time of suffering as well as peace in the midst of pain.

Tremendous new generativity and creativity are experienced during the fifth level. One takes on the whole world as a project to which one contributes one's unique gifts.

Another characteristic of persons at this level is their self-initiating, self-directing life. Their union with God is so constant that intuitively they are able to comprehend God's Will in their regard. Another way of expressing this is a complete openness to the Holy Spirit and a meekness in uniting their will with the Will of God. Many mistakes of course will be made, but no big deal is made of them. They are simply and humbly admitted and accepted and then forgotten without any wasted energy crying over spilt milk. Because of this complete openness, persons at this level do not need the close guidance of spiritual direction that is needed at the lower levels of faith. What a person at the fifth level needs most of all is a soul-friend with whom one can share one's life and activities. Such a soul-friend will be able to give the needed objectivity and accountability that a spiritual director is supposed to furnish. Persons at this level also need a support group of peers to whom one can go for help when experiencing undue stress or overwork. Because a person at this level takes on the whole world as one's project, there is the constant danger of attempting more than one's strength allows. If a support group of peers is available, the needed relief can be obtained when one becomes overextended.

The prayer life of persons at this level will be centered exclusively on God's Will, God's needs, God's Kingdom, and God's plans. Personal needs are no longer the center of one's attention, however, they are not forgotten. The greatest personal need for those at this level is to discern the Will of God in their regard. This discernment is attained through an openness to the Holy Spirit especially as found in the Gospels and other appropriate parts of the Bible. A person at this level is constantly searching in the Sacred Scriptures for those "Ah-ha" verses that reveal

God's Will. Their prayer periods are divided between personal reflection and application of the Bible and periods of quiet resting in the love of God. This marks the beginning of what St. Teresa calls passive contemplation. Great freedom and spontaneity in the choice of prayer is experienced, along with an openness to new, unique ways of prayer taught directly by God. The thought of God becomes the warp and woof of every activity and almost every moment of the day and night.

Spiritual direction for persons at the fifth level consists primarily of two things: total surrender to God and social justice or concern for the welfare of the whole world. A person at this level wants constantly to know how to make a more total surrender to God's Will, God's Spirit, and how to make the greatest possible contribution to needs of the whole of creation. A good spiritual director or soul-friend will lead souls at the fifth level into a greater and greater experience of love of God and neighbor. By increasing one's love for God, others, and even oneself, one is able to neutralize and counteract the negativity of evil in the world and make a positive contribution to the Kingdom of God on Earth.

Sixth Level of Faith

This is the second stage of the Unitive Way that Hall-Tonna calls the Mystical Cycle. Fowler, Kohlberg, and Erikson see this sixth level as the highest of all. Universalizing Faith is the name Fowler gives to it, Kohlberg speaks of Universalizing Principles of Morality, while Erikson speaks of Integrity versus Despair. Saudreau calls persons at this level Heroic Christians while St. Teresa of Avila says that the Sixth Mansion marks the moment of Espousals between the Risen Lord Jesus and a soul. This is also the time of the Dark Night of the Soul described by St. John of the Cross. Global consciousness and Social Justice concerns so totally dominate one's attention that little or no thought is given to one's own needs. Following the example of Jesus as described by St. Paul in the second chapter of Philippians, persons at this level truly adopt the same attitude and mind as that of Jesus Christ. They become willing to assume the burdens of the whole world and become its savior by nonviolent love and victimhood. According to St. Paul, "I am now rejoicing in my sufferings for your sake, and in my flesh I am completing what is lacking in Christ's afflictions for the sake of his body, that is, the church" (Col 1:24).

Persons at this level have attained that balance and integration for which they struggled throughout the fifth level. They become open to the Holy Spirit and the Collective Unconscious but with the proper control so that they are able to govern the release of its energies into their conscious life. There is a radical actualization of the inner self with all of its powers and energies. There is an enlarged, comprehensive vision of reality and truth with a readiness to work for the transformation of the present world into the kingdom of God. One adopts the whole human race as one's peer group and community to the extent of being willing to sacrifice one's life for anyone in the whole world. At this level one is heedless of self-preservation and welfare of self. A detachment from one's needs is experienced that is similar to the example of Jesus in the Gospels. A simple, open, lucid way of life is followed.

Persons at this level of faith are often seen as subversives of present structures and institutions of society. They pose a constant threat to those who favor the status quo. They arouse the opposition of the world in the same way that Jesus did, to the extent that many persons at this level of faith suffer a violent death at the hands of their fellow citizens. However, they will show the same love and nonviolence toward their persecutors as did Jesus on Good Friday. Like Jesus, they have discovered that the way to eliminate evil in the world is not through violence but through victimhood. Instead of using violence to slay the dragon of evil, they allow the dragon to slay them. It is the paradox of the cross. Like Jesus, such persons are able to change the course of history and influence large numbers of people. Two examples of persons at this level in our time are Mohandas Gandhi and Martin Luther King Jr. Both of them were assassinated, both changed the course of history.

Persons at this level possess so much power that there is always the danger of it going to their heads in self-inflation and development of a Messiah Complex. This occurs when they forget that the power they possess is not their own but belongs to God. Whereas, when they misuse their powers for selfish purposes, they can do just as much harm as good. We might think of Satan or the anti-Christ as someone who attains this sixth or seventh level of maturity but deliberately chooses to use their great powers and many skills for evil instead of for good. Persons at this level must avoid too much attention to self-preservation and instead seek to integrate every detail of their life with God.

It is only rare individuals who attain either the sixth or seventh levels of faith. Persons at this level need spiritual guidance to give them the needed objectivity to prevent their power from going to their head. Even though the director may be at a lower level of faith than the directee, it is still possible to give worthwhile guidance to a person at the sixth level. Besides objectivity, the director gives the needed accountability to another human being that everyone should have. It is indeed an awesome responsibility to be the director of someone at the sixth or seventh levels of faith but should the opportunity present itself, one should not refuse to give such guidance.

A person at this level needs to keep a good balance between contemplation and action. Through passive contemplation God is able to pray through one's body, mind, and heart. By such prayer God takes over the total conduct of one's life. In the so-called Espousals a giant step is taken toward the mystical marriage between God and the soul that occurs at the seventh level. One of the results of these Espousals is an openness to all the gifts of the Holy Spirit, especially Knowledge and Understanding. One is now able to read the signs of the times and discern God's plan for the whole of his creation. Thus one becomes a wise enabler and servant leader among other creative, insightful people. One is now ready and able to work for the transformation of the whole world into a more transcendental reality, the kingdom of God.

The likelihood is that few of us will attain the sixth or seventh levels of faith. Nevertheless, we should do all in our power to help and encourage others to attain this sixth level as well as help those who have already arrived at the sixth and seventh levels. We can help such persons by our prayers, love, and encouragement should we come in contact with them. Even though we may never directly encounter persons at the sixth level, they can benefit from our help by our sending out waves of love, prayer, grace, and spiritual power in their direction. We don't need to specify the recipients of our love and prayer but simply pray for those at these highest levels. Since one such person at the sixth or seventh level is capable of changing the course of world history, we will help millions when we help them.

Seventh Level of Faith

Hall-Tonna calls this the Prophetic Cycle. Brian Hall claims that Kohlberg, Erikson, and Fowler fail to treat of this highest level of faith. This is understandable in view of the fact that only the rarest individual attains this level during life on Earth. Abbe Saudreau expresses such rarity by calling persons at this level the Great Saints. St. Teresa of Avila describes the seventh Mansion as Spiritual Marriage between the three Persons of the Blessed Trinity and the human soul. St. Ignatius of Loyola describes this level as the third degree of humility. The desire to become totally Christ-like is so complete that one wishes to suffer the same insults and persecution as did Jesus. St. Francis of Assisi would be a good example of someone at this level. Pope John XXIII is a perfect example of someone who had reached the seventh level of faith. Almost everything stated here regarding the seventh level is seen in the life of John XXIII.

One of the most notable characteristics of a person at this seventh level is the ability to circle all the way back to the first level and both appreciate and experience the values of all seven levels. Thus a person at this level becomes a wise and tremendous enabler to help those at all the other levels bring out the best of which they are capable. A person at this level is capable of attaining great influence over the world and over the whole human race. Along with persons at the sixth level, those at this level truly alter the course of human history. By means of their transcendent union with God, they are able to comprehend the divine and the infinite as well as the finite and smallest human detail with great sensitivity. They look at the world from a "We" perspective that considers both the plans of God as well as the needs of every creature.

In today's world a person at this seventh level will be especially concerned with world peace and the alleviation of world poverty, because these are two of the greatest needs facing us today. They are willing to accept a limited responsibility for the evils, injustices, and oppression in the world and are ready to do all in their power to remedy these evils. Because of their union with God, they are able to take authority for the created order of the world and are ready to sacrifice themselves for its sake. They have a concern for both the largest and the smallest details of God's creation just as God himself has. Because of their love, sympathy, and understanding, they are able to help each person attain the maximum actualization of one's potential for good. As wise, prophetic enablers they are able to engender great enthusiasm in anyone who is willing to work as a team with them. They accept others wherever they happen to be and help them to make a positive contribution to the overall goals and purposes of the world, the church, the country, and society. Because the task is too immense to be accomplished alone, they enlist the help of others to cooperate with God in establishing a just, balanced order in the world. They work always as a team and never alone.

According to Brian Hall the goals for persons at the seventh level are wisdom, transcendence, equality, unity, and perfect love. The means to attain these goals are simplicity, the prophetic word, and total sacrifice of self in love for others. The result will be what St. Teresa calls the *spiritual marriage,* an intimate union with God that maintains both a great intimacy with God as well as compassion for all fellow humans who are in need. One takes responsibility for the world in the same way that Jesus did and endeavors to do all in one's power to save it.

The main danger to be avoided at this level is to allow oneself to become too highly stressed under the burden of the world's problems. Such stress results from an attempt to take over God's job as creator. The expression "Let go, let God" is appropriate for persons at all seven levels, but especially to be remembered at the seventh level. If a person at this level forgets one's place as a creature, there will be an attempt to make over the world according to one's own image instead of the image of God. Such a misuse of power will lead directly to demonic possession and the attempt to personally dominate and control the world and the lives of others.

The prayer form most appropriate for a person at the seventh level is the "We" prayer, whereby one becomes the spokesperson for the whole of creation before the throne of God. One may think of oneself as being united with the Lord Jesus in offering to God the prayers, works, and sufferings of the whole human race. As such a representative, every possible type of prayer will be appropriate at the seventh level: praise, adoration, gratitude, contrition, and petition. Probably, the prayer that best expresses the attitude of a person at the seventh level is the Our Father.

Spiritual direction for a person at the seventh level will be similar to that for the sixth level: objectivity and accountability. Because of the rarity of persons at this seventh level, there is little likelihood that any of us will be asked to give spiritual direction to a person at this level. However, as for those at the sixth level, all of us can send out prayer and love to anyone in the whole world who has reached this level, asking God to protect them and help them do as much good as they can.

Bernadette Roberts, a modern mystic, claims that there are four additional levels of faith beyond the seven levels that St. Teresa of Avila describes. Jesus Christ experienced each of these levels and Christians are called by God to experience these same four levels either during our life on Earth or after death. They are the experiences of abandonment by God at death, descent into the void of hell, resurrection, and ascension. See the three books by Bernadette Roberts: *The Experience of No-Self: A Contemplative Journey, The Path to No-Self: Life at the Center,* and *What Is Self?: A Study of the Spiritual Journey in Terms of Consciousness.*

Conclusion

God is able to make a saint of people at any of the seven levels of faith. Nevertheless, it behooves each of us to grow in faith and attain as high a level as possible, since the higher the level of faith the more power for good we will have. Because we need the help of others to grow in faith, each of us should be ready and willing to give spiritual guidance to anyone who seeks our help and is willing to accept our help. The ministry of spiritual direction enables us to increase manifold the good we are able to accomplish on Earth. The higher the level of faith of those we direct, the more God will use them to carry out his plans for the human race: the coming of God's kingdom.

CHAPTER 11

Four Steps of Individuation

Carl Jung gives the name *individuation* to psychological wholeness and maturity. He insists that every individual person has a unique destiny that is different from every other person. There are certain basic rules to be followed by everyone in order to attain wholeness, but each person has to discover and follow the unique path that is in accord with the way God has created us and the particular destiny God has chosen for us. This teaching of Jung is totally in accord with Christian teaching that says that God has a special, unique relationship of love with each one of us.

Jungian Psychology and Spiritual Guidance

The insights of Jung have been more help to me in giving spiritual direction than the insights of any other single author. I don't agree with several of his conclusions, but for the most part, his ideas are most valuable for those helping others on their journey of faith. Nearly all the suggestions that Jung gives for psychological growth are equally applicable to growth in grace and holiness. Jung has broken down the barriers between nature and grace and between the natural and supernatural.

Jungian psychology and spiritual guidance have a some-what different goal and objective. The goal of Jungian psychology is wholeness or psychological maturity. It emphasizes authenticity, balance, and the actualization of all our human potential for growth. The goal of Christian spiritual guidance is a total openness to God and the Will of God. It is the perfect fulfillment of the three commandments of love: God, neighbor, and self. It has as its goal a personal intimacy with Jesus. Ideally, it would be wonderful if all these goals could be fulfilled. Psychological maturity is a wonderful help to Christian sanctity. However, God never asks the impossible, but only that we do the best we can with the limited talents and energy at our disposal. Many saints were neurotic and had to contend with various psychological hang-ups.

During most of its past history, Christianity has struggled with the opposition between nature and grace that St. Augustine bequeathed to us. Following Plato's opposition between matter and spirit, Augustine and many of the Church Fathers saw nature as the enemy of grace. Jung has shown that basically nature has an identical goal for human beings as does grace. Jung calls it wholeness and insists that we have mistranslated Matthew 5:48. The correct translation for the Greek word *teleios* is not *perfect* but *whole*. Jesus commands us to be whole just as God is whole. Holiness is wholeness as Father Josef Goldbrunner explains in his little book *Holiness Is Wholeness*. A natural, psychologically whole person will also be a holy person. Grace is not opposed to nature but simply gives us special help to fulfill our God-given destiny.

Almost without exception the many suggestions that Jung makes in his books regarding the road to psychological wholeness are the very same ones that Jesus gives us in the Gospels. Fritz Kunkel in his book *Creation Continues* shows how Jung's psychology and Jesus' teachings in the Gospel of Matthew are actually saying the same thing but in different language. We can say that Jung's psychology is a modern updating of much of the teachings of Christianity. The incarnation of God in the human nature of Jesus proves that matter and spirit are not contradictory but must be kept united rather than separated. Jung's psychology helps us do this.

According to Jung there are four basic steps that everyone must take in order to arrive at individuation. They are authenticity, significance, transparency, and solidarity. These four steps correspond with the four basic relationships of love we must bring to maturity in order to become a whole, holy person. *Authenticity* is concerned with a proper relationship of love and knowledge of ourselves. *Significance* deals with a proper relationship with God. *Transparency* describes the right attitude we must have in our relationships of love with other individuals. *Solidarity* is Jung's term to describe the right relationship of love with the various communities to which an individual belongs. All of our life we need to work at all four of these relationships, but, according to Jung, there is a proper order to be followed if we wish to become the individuated and whole person that God and nature have destined for each of us.

Authenticity

Before we can have a good relationship with God and other human beings, we need to have at least the beginning of authenticity regarding ourselves. This basically means being totally honest with ourselves. We must never lie to ourselves about the true state of our person nor pretend to others that we are different from what we truly are. In this sense, honesty and truth are more important than goodness because it is impossible to be truly good unless we are also honest. Jung insists that most of us frequently lie to ourselves as well as to others, often without even being aware of it. Because of fear, insecurity, or other less worthy motives we often pretend to be someone different from what we really are, so that now we are unable to distinguish truth from falsehood when considering who we are.

Because authenticity is so basic to wholeness and maturity and most people are somewhat lacking in authenticity, Jung spent most of his life devising methods of healing and therapy to help us become authentic. His insights regarding persona, shadow, projection, complexes, neuroses, and dreams are primarily designed to help us become truly authentic. The Christian term for authenticity is *humility*. Spiritual writers have traditionally identified humility with honesty and truth and have insisted that humility is the foundation for all the other virtues. Without humility every other virtue is more or less a farce. This explains why Jesus was so strong in his condemnation of the hypocrisy of the Pharisees. The first step toward humility and authenticity is to have the intense desire to be honest and readiness to pay any price to attain it. Ideally, one should have a good hold on authenticity by the age of twenty-eight.

Significance

This is the term Jung uses to describe a good, healthy relationship with God. Jung claimed that we need to be an adult in order to discover our true significance with God and in God's plans for us. He also claimed that persons who fail to discover their significance regarding their relationship with God by the age of thirty-five or forty will almost invariably become sick mentally and psychologically. He said that of all the hundreds of mentally ill patients who came to him for therapy from all over the world, there was not a single one over the age of forty whose problem was not primarily their failure to have a proper relationship with God. To become spiritually healthy, we need to discover our true significance in the overall plan of God. We need to realize that each of us is special to God.

Transparency

In order to experience a mature relationship of love with other individuals, both of the same and the opposite sex, we must be willing to be open, vulnerable, and transparent to those individuals. We thereby risk being hurt, rejected, and taken unfair advantage of. But, according to Jung, this is the only way to experience a true union of love with other human beings. This is the price to be paid for experience of love.

Solidarity

Jung was of the opinion that most people understand how to relate to community only in the second half of life, after the age of forty-five or fifty. The reason for this is that in order to have good community relationships its members need to have had many experiences of need and help, experiences of creatureliness, and experiences of guilt. We need to have been both on the receiving end and giving end of "need and help." We need to be vividly aware of our limitations as creatures. We need to have many experiences of trial and error, of failure, and of mistakes and guilt.

There are specific tasks to be accomplished in each of these four steps of individuation. These tasks change as we progress through life from birth to death. It is important for our spiritual growth that we work at the specific tasks proper to each period of our life. If we fail to accomplish the tasks assigned to an earlier period of life, these tasks do not go away. They now need to be accomplished along with the new tasks assigned to the present period of life. A neglect of spiritual and psychological growth in earlier periods piles up on the tasks of the later periods until the burden of spiritual growth in wholeness becomes well nigh overwhelming. Therefore, let us take a look at the tasks assigned to each twenty-one-year period of our life. We will do this for each of the four steps of individuation.

Stages of Authenticity

Ages 0–21

• Developing the mind, will, imagination, memory, emotions; educating the conscious faculties; building up strong ego and strong will by self-discipline, self-denial, sacrifice, and suffering.

• Gaining knowledge of one's strengths and limitations; honesty, openness to truth of one's faults as well as one's virtues.

• Acquiring self-confidence, self-worth, self-esteem.

• Developing the ideals of super-ego, worshiping of good heroes, dreaming of whom one would like to be.

• Learning how to conform to the expectations of others yet testing newfound gift of freedom and independence.

• Learning how to handle failure, faults, suffering, pain, disappointment.

Ages 21–42

• Developing a good relationship between the conscious ego and the unconscious inner self so that the ego becomes the executive officer who daily makes contact with inner self in order to carry out the Will of God as revealed to the inner self.

• Reinstating the inner, unconscious self as the center of one's life instead of the conscious ego.

• Being open to the vast energies of the inner being of both personal unconscious and collective unconscious.

• Letting go of daydreams of childhood and willingness to live with reality of life and world.

• Learning to stand alone amid the struggles of life in today's world.

• Enduring constant self-assessment in order to find answer to question: "Who am I really?"

• Reconciling freedom and independence with intimacy, whether to choose isolation or intimacy.

• Resolving one's persona; distinguishing roles one plays from our real self.

• Accepting one's limitations and strengths.

• Recognizing one's shadow and taking seriously the interpretation of one's dreams.

• Learning how to open and close the Pandora's box of unconscious archetypes.

• Learning how to resolve one's complexes and neurotic hang-ups.

• Overcoming fear, insecurity, an inferiority complex through development of a proper self-esteem and good self-image.

Ages 42–63

• Discovering one's true and whole destiny and purpose of life on Earth.

• Continuing daily journey of ego into unconscious in order to allow the inner self to be true master of one's life.

• Making decisions regarding the direction to go with one's energies during the second half of life. Shall my life be focused on myself and the satisfaction of the three "Ps" (possessions, pleasure, power) or on altruism in devoting my life's energies to helping others?

• Shifting from physical to the spiritual values of life.

• Resolving the many complexes (distorted archetypes) of one's unconscious inner being.

Ages 63–84

• Accepting the diminishments of aging.

• Finding new, inner resources in quiet prayer and contemplation.

• Developing a peaceful, joyful solitude in preparation for death and life beyond death.

• Realizing that being becomes more important than doing.

• Being content to allow the example of one's authenticity to assist others in their growth to wholeness.

• Learning to live with the memories of the past; accepting one's failures, faults, and willing to forgive self and accept God's forgiveness.

Stages of Significance

Ages 0–21

• Acquiring an appreciation of one's uniqueness as a child of God and God's personal love for one as an individual.

• Appreciating one's dignity as a child of God and member of the Body of Christ.

• Forming a relationship of love with God rather than servile fear.

• Developing awareness and experience of God's love for us.

• Having good experiences of making the needed sacrifices of one's selfishness in order to please God.

• Engaging in personal prayer, family prayer, community and liturgical prayer.

• Experiencing of the truth of Romans 8:28: "We know that all things work together for good for those who love God, who are called according to his purpose."

• Experiencing the simple faith of childhood and adolescent faith.

• Developing a good relationship with God as a loving parent.

• Achieving a balanced faith in the awesome and fascinating aspects of God's nature and a balance between transcendence of God and immanence of God.

• Developing both reverence and intimacy with God.

• Experiencing the two basic gifts of the Holy Spirit: fear of the Lord and piety.

Ages 21–42

• Discovering one's true significance and importance in the overall plan of God; making a sincere effort to be faithful to one's God-given tasks in life.

• Having a good experience of fourth level of adult faith whereby one learns to trust one's own conscience and is willing to break away from strict conformity to the faith and direction of others.

• Forming a relationship with Jesus as a friend, brother, fellow traveler in our journey of faith.

• Experiencing adult conversion of our whole life to God.

• Using adult freedom to make a total commitment of one's life and whole being to God.

Ages 42–63

• Experiencing the fifth level of faith whereby one rethinks and reconstructs all the assumptions of faith as an adult.

• Finding one's place in the building up of the Body of Christ and the institutional church.

• Enduring first-hand experiences with death of loved ones and adult decision regarding one's own death and life after death with God.

• Acquiring an adult appreciation of one's uniqueness and significance in God's plans for this world.

• Having a willingness to use these unique gifts to further God's kingdom.

Ages 63–84

• Experiencing the sixth and seventh levels of faith.

• Experiencing contemplation and mystical union with God.

• Developing a rapport with the Holy Spirit and the gifts and fruits of the Holy Spirit.

• Developing an appreciation of one's true significance in God's kingdom on Earth.

• Learning to be at home with being rather than doing.

• Reconciling of the memories of past sins, faults, failures by an experience of God's merciful forgiveness and love.

• Experiencing frequent dress rehearsals of death in preparation for meeting God, my judge at the moment of death.

• Having the desire to love God perfectly and purely on Earth.

• Willing to spend eternity doing good on Earth.

• Having an appreciation of Communion of Saints and union of living and dead in Risen Lord Jesus.

Stages of Transparency

Ages 0–21

• Innocence of childhood changes at puberty when one becomes insecure and loses childhood innocence.

• The beginning of a persona, a mask of falseness whereby one pretends to be more secure, more capable, and more intelligent that what is actually true.

• One feels pulled between the two poles of freedom and spontaneity on one side and need to conform to peer pressure on the other side.

• One is afraid to be too open lest one be hurt by rejection.

• There is need of many good experiences of being loved unselfishly by parents, teachers, and elders.

• Allowance must be made for the making of many mistakes as the young person gradually learns the art of true, unselfish love of others.

• The beginning of development of one or more of four gender archetypes of mother-father, girl-boy, heroine-fighter, medium-wisdom figure.

Ages 21–42

• One appreciates the need of a mutual sharing of love in order to experience a valid friendship.

• One learns to make a commitment of oneself to another person (marriage, friendship).

• One becomes responsible for the welfare of others (spouse, children).

• One grows in forgetfulness of oneself and becomes sincerely open to others in a true relationship of love.

• One has adult experiences of going out in unselfish love to others.

- One sincerely desires and strives for what is best for others and desires others to show a similar, reciprocal love.
- Transparency of love requires the four steps of knowledge of beloved, self-revelation, mutual benevolence toward the beloved, and union of two lovers.
- One learns how to sustain fidelity of love for others, and how to handle rejection, the breaking down of relationship of love, and disenchantment at failure of beloved to live up to one's hopes and desires.
- Willing to risk transparency and rejection in openness of love to others.
- The development of unconscious archetypes of anima/animus leads to an androgynous union of conscious masculinity and femininity.
- There is a further development of the four gender archetypes.

Ages 42–63

- Releasing from shackles of anxiety and worry concerning the faithfulness of beloved and learning how to enjoy present moment and present experiences of love relationship.
- Learning to broaden the transparency of one's love to include every member of human race.
- Overcoming racial and gender prejudices and becoming truly a protector to the whole world.
- Widening the circle of love for others and willing to suffer many rejections and being taken unfair advantage by those to whom one has freely opened one's heart in love.

Ages 63–84

• One no longer feels the need to beg for the admiration of others but is able to stand solidly in one's own truth and past experiences of love.

• One no longer concerned about selfish attainments, no longer competitive with others but open and transparent in love for all.

• One reaps the benefits of transparency by enjoying the experience of many deep love relationships with individuals of both sexes.

• One now has the ability to stand-alone without going to pieces when the beloved dies or a friendship is lost.

• One is able to live on the memories of previous love given and received.

Stages of Solidarity

Ages 0–21

• Having good family relationships with parents and siblings.

• Having good experiences with peer groups in school, play, work; learning to share with others at home, play, school, playground, kindergarten, grade school, high school, sports, college.

• Respecting the rights of others, disciplining one's selfish desires.

• Learning responsibility for others, taking care of others, especially those who are younger, weaker and unable to take care of themselves.

• Taking responsibility for environment, care of planet, ecology, welfare of the whole human race and other living things, resources.

• Experiencing a growing sense of oneness with the whole of creation, whole human race, and the whole world.

Ages 21–42

• One helps others in need and experiences many personal needs that can only be relieved by the help of others.

• Through these many experiences of need and help, one comes to an understanding of the solidarity of the whole human race and whole of creation.

• This sense of oneness with others is often experienced when one risks one's own life and welfare in order to help another person, perhaps a total stranger.

• Through the experience of personal guilt for some harm to others that can no longer be rectified, one comes to an appreciation of our creatureliness and our need of mutual forgiveness of our faults.

• One develops altruism for the welfare of the whole human race and whole earthly planet.

• One has ecological concerns for future of our planet.

• One assumes responsibility for welfare of the world and walks in the shoes of others in order to develop empathy for others needs.

• There is a recognition of freedom of others to make their own ethical and religious choices as long as they do not destroy the rights of others.

• One overcomes racial and gender prejudices.

• One learns to work with all the communities to which one belongs.

• One takes intelligent interest in politics and willingness to make a contribution to good government.

Ages 42–63

- One recognizes one's responsibility to future generations of human race and is ready to adopt a more simple lifestyle in order to preserve the Earth for those who will come after us.
- One begins to realize how one fits into whole community of human race.
- There is a recognition of the evil and foolhardiness of war and violence.
- One strives for peace and end of war and violence.
- One looks for a just distribution of the goods and resources of the world to all the peoples on Earth.
- One experiences a willingness to make a substantial contribution to the welfare of the world even at a great cost to oneself.

Ages 63–84

- There is a stepping back from leadership and willingness to pass the baton of leadership to the younger generation.
- One shares wisdom and experience with others, especially the young.
- One rejoices at success of others just as much as with one's own successes.
- There is a sense of oneness with the whole of creation, whole of reality.
- One makes the needs of others equal or even of greater importance than one's own needs. "No one has greater love than this, to lay down one's life for one's friends" (John 15:13).

CHAPTER 12

Spiritual Direction
in Times of Crisis

One of the most important times when spiritual direction is needed is during a *crisis*. Webster's dictionary defines a crisis as a decisive moment, a turning point, a crucial time. It comes from the Greek word *krino* that means to separate. Therefore, it refers to any critical moment in our lives when we have to make a decision to go either one way or the other. We can no longer continue to go the old way. Father Josef Goldbrunner suggests that approximately once every seven years the average person experiences a crisis in one's life. During the intervening years there will be minor crises to face, but it is the decisions we make in these major, seven-year crises that primarily determine the course of our life, whether we continue to grow in holiness and wholeness or instead regress to a more infantile way of life.

One must not be too literal in thinking of these major crises as occurring exactly every seven years. One needs to allow a cushion of one or two years on each side of the seven-year cycle. Also, not everyone follows exactly this seven-year cycle. There will be numerous exceptions. But in order to see if this suggestion may have value, look back over one's life at the ages of 7–14–21–28–35–42–49–56–63–70 to see if around those years, give or take a year or two, one did have to make a major decision regarding the direction of one's life. Regardless of its accuracy, this will be a convenient way to list the major crises that face most people. Spiritual direction has great value at these times and there is a different kind of direction needed for each crisis. The actual crisis may continue over a period of months or even years, so that not just one decision but many decisions will be needed.

Adolescence (14)

Besides the obvious problems connected with puberty, this is the first time in life that a person becomes free to make decisions about life in general. This is the first time one is capable of making an adult commitment to God and experience an adult religious conversion. This is a very critical time because this is the time when a young person makes those very important decisions about one's general attitude toward life, self, others, and God. One of the most important decisions of this period is the willingness to sacrifice "play" as the major interest in one's life and accept the seriousness of purpose necessary to become a mature adult. One of the greatest dangers for adolescents is to cling to the illusions and dreams of childhood and refuse to face the difficult facts of the world and life as they actually exist.

Before becoming a teenager, one is governed mostly by impulse, and the average child has few real problems. Children living in dysfunctional families will have considerably greater difficulties in making the needed decisions at adolescence. If the teenager has a poor self-image and is filled with insecurity, inner fears, and lack of trust in God or other human beings, there is danger that such a person will continue to cling obsessively to the old ways of childhood and refuse to face the challenges of adulthood. Whereas if the teenager has had many experiences of unselfish love received and given, plus a willingness to work hard and sacrifice oneself for the good of others, there is good reason to expect a good decision to leave the carefree years of childhood and accept adult responsibilities.

Growth in self-consciousness makes a teenager aware of one's own power, freedom, and value as a person. If one's parents and elders are unwilling to allow this budding of adulthood to mature, the inevitable conflicts between teenager and parents or adults will result. On the other hand, lack of experience, especially an absence of failure, often makes the teenager over-optimistic about chances of success and causes one to underestimate the difficulties and struggles needed to succeed. Parents who try to satisfy every desire of their children are doing a disservice to these children. Life thrives and matures when there is a good balance of pleasure and pain, hardship and ease, self-denial and self-indulgence, failure and success. Life withers and growth in maturity is brought to a halt when there is too much of either pleasure or pain, failure or success, hardship or ease. This is frequently the tragedy of children from dysfunctional families.

If one has had good experiences of receiving and giving unselfish love during the previous years of childhood, the teenager will find it less difficult to learn the complicated art of loving and being loved by others, especially those of the other sex. Even in the most favorable circumstances, the teenager needs to exercise much discipline, self-denial, and self-control in order to bring to maturity the awakening powers of sex and love. Until now these powers have remained dormant within the depths of the inner being. Many difficulties can be expected as the budding adult struggles with one's awakened sexuality. Sex becomes extremely fascinating and arouses curiosity. A tremendous attraction is felt for the other sex to complement one's one-sided personality. The newly awakened perception of the hidden value of persons and things along with the feeling of personal freedom and independence contribute to the seriousness of the crises that mark this particular stage of growth.

A teenager needs a good support group of peers to take the place of the authority of the parents that is now gradually abandoned. One is still too insecure, inexperienced, and limited in knowledge to be able to stand alone or trust one's own conscience. The most serious crisis facing a teenager is to find and choose a trustworthy peer group on whom one can depend to help make the right decisions regarding the present and future conduct of one's life. This is also the age of hero worship. If some mature, unselfish adult can gain the confidence of the teenager, this may spell the difference between success or failure at this critical period of life. Such an adult may be an athletic coach, a teacher, a clergy person, a school counselor, or just some wise, adult friend other than the father or mother.

Adulthood (21)

The main crisis facing one at this period of life is the cutting of the psychological umbilical cord that has kept the teenager still connected to one's family. This often happens after graduation from high school when one leaves home to go to college or to take a job that requires one to live apart from the family homestead. Legally, we speak of a person "coming of age" at one's twenty-first birthday.

Youth ends and adulthood begins when one is ready and willing to take hold of one's future destiny, assume full responsibility for one's life, and makes some kind of commitment of life's energies to some ideal or person. This is the time when one makes a specific dedication of life to a particular profession, vocation, or cause. Similarly it is the usual time that one makes a commitment of self to a particular person in marriage. This is to be done regardless of the uncertain consequences.

The more self-discipline one has developed in earlier life, the easier it will be to make this decision that plunges one into adult life. The more generous and unselfish is this decision, the easier and more certain it will be that the right decisions will be made in the many other serious matters that will face one during remainder of one's life.

The first twenty-eight years of one's life should be spent in the education of one's conscious faculties: senses, intellect, will, imagination, memory, feelings. The knowledge of oneself as independent from others begins around the age of two. The training of the conscious faculties and the ego, which is the center of conscious life, continues until a person is ready and willing to make a complete commitment of one's conscious faculties to some cause or person. Those young people who find it necessary to struggle hard to make ends meet materially and physically are usually spared deeper inner problems. Those who are required to make few sacrifices and practice little self-discipline usually find it difficult to assume the responsibilities of adult life. Instead they often remain in a state of permanent childishness or mediocrity throughout their adult years.

The crisis of twenty-one or thereabouts is that one can no longer blame parents or childhood home when things go wrong. Each one now has either to put up or shut up. Having cut the last cords binding one to childhood one is now challenged to create a new home of one's own. As the mistakes pile up, one begins to realize the need of help from others. This is when a good spiritual director can be invaluable. Likewise, a support group of other young adults who are facing similar questions and problems as oneself will enable one to persevere in carving out one's future destiny. This is the time to rectify and develop all that had been neglected in the earlier years. This is often the last opportunity to attain self-control and self-discipline in regard to one's conscious faculties.

Maturing Adulthood (28)

The middle period of one's life from twenty-eight to fifty-six should be the time when one experiences the most psychological growth. Unfortunately, many people imagine that education ends with youth and they think of adulthood as almost exclusively given to activity. If this idea is carried out in practice, not only does psychological and spiritual growth come to a halt, but also a process of regression and return to childish immaturity begins.

During the middle period from twenty-eight to fifty-six, one needs to educate and develop one's unconscious faculties. If the tasks of youth have been successfully accomplished, one is now ready to tackle the even more important tasks of adulthood. These tasks consist of bringing to the level of consciousness the many undeveloped talents, resources, and energies that have remained asleep in the unconscious inner being. The most important of these energies is the power to love. One begins to realize that real love is quite different from the "puppy love" that one has been able to experience up until now. Mature love has four objectives: (1) proper love for one's inner self; (2) proper love and respect for God; (3) proper love and respect for other individual human beings; and (4) proper love and respect for the communities of people to whom one belongs. These four objectives constitute the four stages of psychological and spiritual growth during the middle period of life. All four will require attention throughout the next twenty-eight years.

Carl Jung calls the first of these tasks *authenticity*. It refers to self-knowledge and the gradual uncovering of one's persona and shadow, both positive and negative. The crisis of this period of life is to establish a correspondence between external conduct and one's authentic, inner being. God has implanted deep within one's unconscious the blueprint of one's life's destiny. One must now make many voyages of self-discovery into the unconscious in order to discern one's true destiny and then find the courage to make the needed adjustments in one's conscious life in order to live up to one's vocation.

Adult education means to "lead out" *(educare)* the potential talents and energies stored in our unconscious inner being and use whatever effort required to put them to work in worthwhile causes. We must be willing to empty ourselves of mere self-serving and become servants of humanity. We must be willing to stand solidly in our own truth and not escape into a dream world of nonreality. This is the time to develop those sides of our personality that have previously remained uncultivated. We must learn the necessary skills for interpreting correctly the voice of our unconscious and permit an easy flow of communication between the conscious and unconscious sides of our personality. Thus we become truly masters of our life and experience a tremendous new zest for life, new enthusiasm, and creativity along with a loss of fear and insecurity.

Mature Religious Conversion (35)

Somewhere around the age of thirty-five many people experience a crisis of faith regarding God and religion. No longer is one content with the answers to religious questions that were received in childhood or youth. One needs to demythologize the former faith assumptions and find adult answers to the mysteries of God and religion. If one succeeds in finding reasonable answers to one's doubts and questions, there will be an experience of a mature religious conversion. Such an experience may come at any point in one's adult life, but quite frequently it occurs sometime between the ages of thirty and forty. Carl Jung claimed that if one reaches the age of forty without having experienced this mature religious conversion, one usually experiences some form of mental illness. A true religious conversion occurs when one chooses to believe in a personal God who loves us and cares for us. The Christian makes a further leap of faith to believe that God became a human being in the person of Jesus. The final act of faith is a complete gift of self in love to this loving God.

Mid-Life Crisis (42)

By the age of forty-two half of one's life on Earth is over, yet few persons have accomplished half of the goals, plans, dreams, ambitions, and hopes that one had at the age of twenty-one or twenty-eight. Perhaps for the first time in life one comes face to face with the reality of one's own death and the end of life here on Earth. To prevent oneself from going into a tailspin, one needs to readjust one's goals and ambitions and set new sights that are spiritual and not dependent on mere earthly life. Without a strong belief in God and in life after death, a person at this age can become depressed and lose all hope. For parents who have been previously busy raising a family, they realize that soon their children will no longer need them. For those who have chosen a worldly career, they begin to realize that they will never fulfill all their youthful ambitions.

Many men and women at this age stick their head in the sand and pretend the aforementioned facts are not true. By ignoring their reality, they think the problems will go away. All they do is postpone the inevitable day when their dreamworld comes crashing down around them. The younger one is when hit by the realization of one's creatureliness, the better chance one has of readjusting life's goals more realistically.

The main task facing every person during their forties is to learn to love others in a fully mature way. Having learned to confide in God during the thirties, one is now ready to confide in other human beings. There is always the risk of our love being rejected and abused when we make a gift of self to another person. Yet, we must take this chance if we are to keep growing in maturity. Through the experience of human love given and received, many repressed areas of our unconscious will be discovered and developed. When these relationships are with persons of the other sex, the most observable development will be a good balance between masculinity and femininity in one's whole life.

One is capable of mature "I-Thou" relationships of love only after successfully completing the previous tasks of self-discipline, centering of one's life in one's inner self, and the commitment of one's life to God or some higher cause than one's own selfish needs. For this reason a really mature adult relationship of love usually develops only after the age of forty. Sometimes, but not necessarily, such mature relationships occur with those with whom we have established youthful relationships. Thus serious problems of relationship frequently develop with married people between the ages of forty and fifty. Blessed indeed are those couples who "find each other" and fall in love all over again with the spouse whom they married twenty years previously.

If we refuse to make the sacrifices of selfishness necessary in order to have an experience of mature love, progress in maturity comes to a halt and one begins to regress into some form of childishness and spiritual sterility. There is also a serious regression into mediocrity and selfishness. One becomes prematurely old, barren and dry, hard and brittle, pessimistic and bitter toward life. Some lose hope and withdraw into a shell and cut themselves off from their fellow human beings. Most of the vital energies of growth come to a halt. Idiosyncrasies that used to be seen as humorous, now become a source of irritation to everyone. Such persons often spend their time criticizing and blaming others for all that is wrong in the world, blaming everyone but the real culprit, that is, their own refusal to give themselves in mature love to others. A general pessimism, resentment, and negativism are shown to the whole world.

On the other hand, the middle-aged person who is able to overcome one's selfishness and pride and is willing to go out in unselfish love to others, now experiences a beautiful new growth in character. New powers never previously experienced are now discovered in oneself. Tenderness and sympathy for all those who suffer or are in need is experienced. Being open to others through love opens one to many worthwhile values: God, truth, beauty, religion, and social justice. Instead of discouragement and pessimism, one becomes full of hope for the future. Enthusiasm, creativity, and a noticeable increase of both physical and psychic energy are experienced. By means of love one discovers that fountain of youth for which humankind has been searching from time immemorial.

Second Mid-Life Crisis (49)

Having gained a certain proficiency in individual relationships of love, a person is now better able to establish good community relations. Learning how to get along in community begins at home in the family, then in school, and later at work. In middle age a new crisis of community relationships occurs. Realizing that one will not remain on Earth forever, one needs to step back and look for groups of people who might carry out and accomplish some or all of the worthwhile goals and objectives to which one has been devoting one's previous life. Instead of seeing others as rivals, we must learn to see them as partners on a team. Through the community of our fellow human beings, we can accomplish much more than we could ever do alone. We need now to turn with confidence to these groups of people and entrust the future to them. Through our influence on those younger than ourselves, we confide our dreams and hopes to them. We adopt a sincere confidence in the youth of the next generation.

To attain good community relations we need many experiences of need and help; other's need of our help and our need of other's help. We also need experiences of guilt, of failure, of personal mistakes. This will enable us to be tolerant of the faults and limitations of others.

As we gradually realize our dependence on one another, we realize our solidarity with the whole human race. We realize we are not self-sufficient, not able to do everything ourselves. We learn to put our confidence in the various communities to which we belong rather than in ourselves. Thus we are able to remain optimistic about the future even though we know that we personally will never be able to accomplish all the tasks that need to be done or that we, when younger, had hoped to accomplish personally. The truly mature person is able to share with the whole community all that one has learned, all one's hopes and dreams for the future. Similarly, one is not selfish about one's own accomplishments, but realizes that they belong to the community and not just to oneself. Without the help of many others, we would never have accomplished the things we did. The hallmark of this period of life is the ability to confide, to commit, and to entrust the future to the communities of which one is now a small part.

Mature Adulthood (56)

Unfortunately many people look upon the last third of their life on Earth as their declining years. They imagine that when they reach the age of fifty-six most of their life is over. Actually, if one has successfully carried out the tasks appropriate to each of the previous seven-year cycles, the fullness of life on Earth only begins around the age of fifty-six. The last third of life on Earth is meant to be the most productive, the most happy and fulfilled part of our earthly existence. Having substantially finished the many tasks needed for maturity, one now has the joy of sharing all of one's treasures with others. This then is the beginning of the age of wisdom when others are able to benefit from all we have learned during the previous fifty-six years.

The main crisis facing a person at age of fifty-six is to shift one's goal from "doing" to "being." If one is to spend a fruitful old age, it is essential in the closing years of one's active life to shift attention from busy worldly activity to becoming and being the particular image and reflection of God that each of us has been destined by God to be. This being will consist primarily of a complete forgetfulness of self and the living of an entirely other-centered life. Such an unselfish love will result in a transparency that radiates outward on all who come into contact with such a person. One becomes so transparent that one's light shines on the whole of creation. Pope John XXIII was such a person. It was only in his old age that people finally recognized the greatness of this man. Yet, all of his earlier life has been a preparation for those few final years of old age when the transparency of his love transformed and revolutionized the Church and the world.

If one has properly solved the previous tasks of maturity, there is no such thing as old age. Through spiritual maturity we become perpetually young, always growing, and open to the infinite riches of that transcendental dimension called God. Those who have cooperated with God's graces and have tried to fulfill the challenges of their unconscious potential will find that the later years of life are not dull but become more interesting and joyful as we advance in years.

Several important tasks face one at the age of fifty-six. First, this is almost the last opportunity to complete any unfinished tasks of earlier life. Such uncompleted tasks don't go away but continue to haunt us and call for our attention as long as we live. Second, now is the time to prepare oneself for retirement by undertaking the needed preparation for some new ministry, one that will be in keeping with one's advanced years and decreasing physical energy. Third, one should continue to gather disciples and persons of the younger generation with whom one can share one's wisdom and experience and to whom one can entrust the carrying on of the work begun by oneself.

Retirement (63)

The crisis of retirement requires the bold facing and acceptance of advancing years, declining strength, and the nearness of death. The more religiously oriented our earlier life was, the less critical will be the moment of retirement. Advanced age has been given to us for the final accomplishment of our religious and psychological perfection. To finish these tasks we need leisure, and God has providentially made this possible through early retirement. Rather than resisting the inactivity of retirement, we should look forward with keen anticipation to these final years of life. Spiritually speaking they can and should be the most active years of our whole life. Therefore, as we lay down the tools of our work, we should have some new task in keeping with our age to keep us busy. In some way this should consist in sharing with others the wisdom and the experience we have gained throughout our life. This is also the time to put together the final edition of our philosophy of life that we can hope to leave as our main heritage to the next generation. The period of retirement from active life should be a period of growth in the unitive and mystical ways of prayer. One's sense of solidarity with the rest of humanity will be so great that one rejoices as much in the good fortune and success of others as if it were one's own.

Preparation for Death (70)

All of life should be a dress rehearsal for death. From youth we need to be keenly aware of how fragile life is and how quickly it can be lost without the slightest forewarning. Throughout life we need to reflect on death and live sufficiently detached from the things of this world so that we are willing to depart without looking back. The older we get and the more we realize that most of our life is behind us, the more foolish we are to act as though we were going to live indefinitely on Earth. If we have lived with the thought of death often enough throughout the earlier years of life, the experience of the diminishments and weaknesses and perhaps pains that warn us of approaching death will not disturb us. Instead, we will look forward with peace and joy to the final consummation of our union with God in the great beyond. We blindly trust our whole future into God's loving care. "Father, into your hands I commend my spirit" (Luke 23:46).

Those who experience a terminal illness at some earlier period of life face a crisis considerably greater than that of older people. The five steps listed by Dr. Elisabeth Kübler-Ross are actually five different crises that most people must resolve when faced with the immanent probability of death. They are: denial, rebellion, bargaining, pleading, and acceptance. Spiritual directors and friends of the terminally ill need to be present and patiently help the suffering person through each of these stages of facing death. There is a different way to minister to the sick person, depending on which phase of acceptance one is experiencing. But the main way to help is by one's presence, love, and acceptance of whatever disposition is currently being manifested. Rather than trying to force or even encourage the person to pass on to the next stage of acceptance, we can best minister to such a person by allowing the providence of God gradually to lead the sick person to final acceptance and peace.

CHAPTER 13

Spiritual Direction for the Different Temperaments

A knowledge of the different temperaments and personality types is not absolutely necessary for spiritual direction, but it is such a tremendous help that a spiritual director would be irresponsible not to make use of this knowledge. Persons of different temperaments vary considerably in the way they respond to God's call to holiness and wholeness. Advice or guidance that is appropriate for one personality may be totally ineffective for a person of another temperament. The more knowledge a director has of the differences between the various temperaments, the better he or she can guide another person, provided also that the directee has been accurately typed. The best tool for typing a person is the Myers-Briggs Type Indicator (MBTI). However, there are other ways to discern one's temperament if the MBTI is not readily available. David Keirsey in his book *Please Understand Me: Character and Temperament Types* gives the Keirsey Temperament Sorter for typing persons. In *Prayer and Temperament,* in Appendix I, pp. 121–26, Marie Norrisey and I offer another method for determining one's personality type.

For understanding how spiritual direction differs for the different temperaments, read chapters 4 to 7 in *Prayer and Temperament.* In these four chapters the characteristics of each of the four temperaments are given and the spirituality appropriate to each temperament is described. In this present chapter a summary of what is found in *Prayer and Temperament* is given along with some additional insights concerning the specific spiritual direction appropriate for each of the four temperaments.

Different authors suggest different names for the four temperaments. In this chapter the two-letter designations are primarily used: NF, SJ, SP, and NT. NF is the acronym for Intuition-Feeling; SJ, for Sensing-Judging; SP, for Sensing-Perceiving; and NT, for Intuition-Thinking. In the subtitle for each of the next four sections, the names used in *Prayer and Temperament* are given, namely, Augustinian, Ignatian, Franciscan, and Thomistic. The comparable names used by David Keirsey in *Please Understand Me,* namely, Apollonian, Epimethean, Dionysian, and Promethean, are given. Third, the traditional names of the four temperaments first used by Hippocrates about 450 B.C. are given. They are Choleric, Melancholic, Sanguine, and Phlegmatic.

The NF (Augustinian, Apollonian, Choleric) Temperament

David Keirsey states that only about 12 percent of the population of this country belongs to this temperament. Nevertheless, the likelihood is that at least half of the persons who seek spiritual direction will be of this temperament. Persons of this temperament have a tremendous drive for self-development and spiritual, psychological growth. Also, usually, persons of this NF temperament make good spiritual directors. Not only are they willing to spend the necessary time and energy for their own spiritual growth, but also they are willing to help others grow spiritually, since they appreciate so much its importance.

The primary motivation for a NF is love. Because of their deep feelings and great sensitivity, they can appreciate God's love for them and can easily be motivated to make as total a return of love to God as possible. They also will understand how their love for God needs to be expressed on Earth by means of their love for their fellow human beings. NFs need many strokes of affirmation and support from the director and should be encouraged to give strokes to others. They prefer cooperation rather than competition. They need acceptance by others; therefore any negativity received from others is deadly for the NF. The director must show them how to handle such negativity and transform it into love. The example of Jesus in his passion where he constantly returned good for evil is the model for the NF to follow. Nonviolence has a great appeal to the NF.

NFs are not good at handling conflict, criticism, and opposition. They blossom when receiving a positive feedback but wither before a negative reaction from another. The director should help the NF find a proper response to make when experiencing opposition or negative criticism. The NF also needs help in learning how to resolve conflicts when they arise. Depression and discouragement are frequently a problem for NFs. A director will need to spend much time helping the NF develop a positive, trusting attitude toward God, oneself, others, the world, and the future. Once the NF is thoroughly convinced of God's great love for them exactly as they are—sins, faults, and all—the temptation to discouragement and depression can usually be resolved.

The NF is constantly searching for meaning, authenticity, integrity, and self-identity. They have a tremendous urge for wholeness, holiness, completeness, personal growth, self-actualization, and personal fulfillment. More than any other temperament, the NF will be interested in depth psychology and how it relates to God and sanctity. The psychology of Carl

G. Jung is especially helpful in finding good answers to the NF's questions about meaning and self-actualization.

Persons are so much more important than things for the NF. For this reason they are usually very good at human relationships especially if they are extroverts. Their intuitive faculty enables them to catch nonverbal communication; therefore they are usually quite good in judging the character and personality of the people they encounter. A spiritual director will need to give special attention in helping the NF use these abilities in a positive rather than negative way.

As explained in chapter 5 of *Prayer and Temperament*, the favorite method of prayer for NFs is to transpose the words of the Gospels and other parts of the Bible to their own situation today. They try to imagine Jesus or the Holy Spirit speaking the words in the Gospel to them in their present situation. By personalizing the gospel message, they make it come alive and meaningful to them today. The Bible becomes a personal letter sent from heaven to them. It is not possible to personalize every verse of the Bible, but a NF will look for the "Ah-ha" verses that seem to be a personal message from God. These then become their favorite texts for prayer and meditation. By activating their Intuitive Function, the NF is able to see the deeper meaning of a scripture text and by means of their Feeling Function, they succeed in personalizing the biblical message.

Because NFs are usually facile in communicating with others both by speaking and writing, the daily use of a spiritual journal should strongly be recommended by the spiritual director. In this way the NF is able to put into order the host of insights that come crowding into their minds from their Intuitive faculty. In addition, a spiritual journal helps them to remember the good ideas that pop into their mind during prayer. A NF may wish to share one's journal with the director, but this should never be imposed by the director, otherwise this may hinder the free expression of one's thoughts while journaling.

A NF becomes terribly upset when treated impersonally. To make sure this does not happen a director must be a good listener whenever the NF speaks and make a special effort to understand clearly what the NF is trying to say. The director can use this same trait of the NF to encourage both a deep personal relationship with God and Jesus Christ as well as encouraging a proper intimacy in the NF's relationships with other human beings.

NFs are highly committed to helping others and relate well to those who befriend them. They are full of empathy, compassion, and understanding for others. They can see possibilities for good in others that the person involved is not aware of. They are able to see good in everyone. They are the natural rescuers of people in trouble. This can lead to the danger of becoming too involved in others' problems. The director needs to keep all this in mind when the directee is a NF.

NFs are able to be very enthusiastic, optimistic, and capable of engendering hope and enthusiasm in others, provided they have succeeded in overcoming their own fears and negativity. They are never content with the present, but always are striving to fulfill the unlimited potential for growth that God has implanted in every one of us. They sometimes set too high a goal for themselves so that they are unable to attain it. The director will need to moderate the NF's enthusiasm and limit the goals the NF wishes to pursue. The NF's discontent with the present and the desire for change may also need to be moderated. An effort should be made to help NFs live primarily in the present, trusting the future to God. Their hunger and thirst for growth, self-development, and self-actualization will be attained by concentrating their energies on God's Will here and now.

Of all the temperaments, prayer comes easiest for the NF. This will explain why most of the books written about prayer and spirituality have been written by NFs. Therefore, they will find an abundance of good literature in today's book market as well as in libraries of past wisdom to satisfy their hunger for greater knowledge about God, prayer, and spirituality. The director will encourage them to be very selective in their spiritual reading and avoid becoming a slave to the book they are currently reading because there is a danger that their enthusiasm will get carried away by the latest insight that they have received.

NFs have a great need for daily periods of quiet and silence in order to make contact with their inner selves and there encounter God. Experiencing a deep, personal relationship with God is the one essential element of any authentic NF spirituality. Daily prayer and quiet are a must for the NF and the director should urge a NF to spend a whole hour of such prayer each day. Without this daily period of prayer, the spiritual life of the NF will wither, fade, and die just as a beautiful flower if it is not watered, nourished, and tended.

The SJ (Ignatian, Epimethean, Melancholic) Temperament

Approximately 38 percent of the general population of this country belongs to the SJ temperament. Probably 50 to 60 percent of the regular church members will be of this temperament. These are the practical, down-to-earth people who have a strong sense of responsibility and duty. They are careful, cautious, conscientious, and very serious in their desire to carry out whatever commitments they have made in the past. Therefore, after the NFs, the SJs will be the group most interested in spiritual direction. Yet the method of directing a SJ will vary considerably from what is recommended for a NF.

While a NF's interest is primarily future oriented and visionary, the SJ's interest is primarily historical and concerned with the past. The favorite method of prayer for the SJ is to project oneself back into the historical event as described in the Gospel or Bible and imagine oneself to be a part of the original event. This is the method of prayer used by the Church in celebrating the different feasts of the Liturgical Year. Each year during the Liturgical Cycle we project ourselves back to the birth of Jesus at Bethlehem; his baptism in the Jordan; his Palm Sunday procession into Jerusalem; and the events of his passion, death, and resurrection. By reliving these events of the past, we try to draw some practical lessons that will help us to know how we should live our life today. This method of prayer is very ancient. It was the method used by the Israelites and still used by the Jews in their yearly Passover celebration. SJs should be encouraged to make the fullest possible use of the liturgy of the Church to help them to grow spiritually. Besides participation in the official Church liturgy, they will find it helpful to build their private, personal prayers and devotions around the events and scripture texts used in the public liturgy.

SJs love to be of service to others. A SJ child can be spotted in the kindergarten class as the one anxious to be teacher's little helper. They are deeply committed to caring for those in need and desire to contribute to the good of society. A great deal of the spiritual direction of the SJ will be involved with the particular choices of loving service that a person should do. There will always be more good to be accomplished than what one is able to fulfill. One of the dangers for a SJ is to become overcommitted and overworked. This temperament has what is called a work ethic. "If I don't do it, who will?" The spiritual director will need to help the SJ know when to say no to another's request for help.

SJs are usually conservative and find changes difficult to handle. They may adhere to Murphy's Law that if anything can go wrong, it surely will. Therefore, they feel more comfortable with the status quo. They are the great stabilizers of society. This can be either good or harmful. The task of the director is to help the directee know when to be faithful to tradition and when it is in the best interests of everyone to leave the past and undertake something new.

SJs are great law-and-order persons and are unable to live in an unplanned or disorderly environment. They take deadlines very seriously and need to follow a schedule. They become very upset when others around them live a disorderly life. Very often a SJ is married to such a person or has such a person as a co-worker. The director will need to spend much time helping the SJ cope with such situations. The law-and-order aspect of the SJ's temperament can be put to good use by encouraging such a person to develop a good Personal Growth Plan and then to follow it seriously. A SJ has a good understanding of accountability and the director at each meeting should ask an accounting of all the resolutions previously made. Such a regular accountability will probably yield more lasting good results than any other thing.

The biblical concept of our relationship with God as a journey of faith is appealing to the SJ. The director needs to point out the continuity between past traditions and any new spiritual exercises recommended to the SJ. The image of a spiral staircase is useful in showing the SJ how one must return again and again to the same six steps of the journey of faith but always at a higher level. A good knowledge of Bible history and whole history of salvation will greatly aid the director and the directee in seeing the continuity of today's recommendations with the best traditions of the past. Nowhere is this more apparent than in the Christian Eucharist as a continuation of the Jewish Passover and Berakah meal. For both Jews and Christians the belief is that each time we remember God's marvelous deeds of the past, we make the same God really and truly present to work similar marvelous deeds for us. Thus the Eucharist makes the past come alive and real, and this has a special appeal for a SJ. Gratitude for past events is very much a part of the SJ person.

One of the greatest needs of the SJ is trust in God, trust in themselves, trust in others, and trust in the future. The SJ is very realistic in recognizing the presence of evil and danger. If this realism is allowed to go too far, the SJ becomes quite negative and pessimistic toward the world, others, the future, and even toward God and themselves. Much of the spiritual direction of a SJ will be occupied in overcoming all negativity and developing a very positive, trustful attitude toward God, others, themselves, the future, and even toward the world. A text of the Bible that will help the SJ attain this trust is Romans 8:28: "We know that all things work together for good for those who love God, who are called according to his purpose." Many of the Psalms express the trust in God that a SJ needs. A good exercise to help the SJ grow in trust would be to go through all 150 Psalms and underline all references to trust in God. Psalm 91 is probably the Psalm most concerned about trust; all but one of its verses is on this theme. The teachings of Jesus in the Gospel frequently emphasize the importance and necessity of trust in God. Often this is translated as faith but almost always it is talking about trust.

The SP (Franciscan, Dionysian, Sanguine) Temperament

According to David Keirsey, there are approximately as many SPs among the population of this country as SJs, about

38 percent. However, the likelihood is that very few SPs will come seeking spiritual direction unless they are experiencing some sort of a crisis. Nevertheless, they have as much need for direction as any other temperament. Therefore, the spiritual director will need to initiate the suggestion for direction among the SPs of one's acquaintance. A SP is usually very generous and loves to respond to a challenge, especially when it involves something difficult. Someone has said that for the SP the impossible just takes a little longer.

The majority of the dropouts from high school, college, the churches, society, will be SPs. They show little loyalty to the institutions to which they belong and vote with their feet when there is no longer anything that interests them. SPs are action persons who want to be free, unconfined, and able to do whatever their spirit moves them to do. Therefore, it is important that the SP be dedicated to God so that this inner spirit is the Holy Spirit and not a merely human spirit or evil spirit. SPs are impulsive and dislike being tied down by rules. It is the task of spiritual direction to help them be totally committed to doing God's Will; otherwise their free spirit will lead them astray.

SPs are considerably different from either the SJ or the NF. The SJ is especially interested in the past, tradition, history. The NF is just as interested in the future and is seen as a visionary or prophet leading us to a future goal. The SP lives very much in the present without concern either for the past or the future. Neither yesterday nor tomorrow exists for a SP. They are always looking for something new—new things to do, new places to go. They thrive on excitement, adventure, risk, and challenge. They hunger for activity and enjoyment. They live life intensively and are capable of unrelenting vigor when excited or challenged. They are usually optimistic, cheerful, light hearted, witty, and charming. The air takes on a glow when a SP enters the room. They bring with them a sense that something exciting is about to happen. They live extensively and are able to survive setbacks, are only temporarily defeated. They are usually easy to get along with, adaptable, flexible, open minded, and willing to change their position. They are unusually good as peacemakers, reconcilers, and conciliators, because in their view almost everything is negotiable. They make good troubleshooters and are good at unsnarling messes, able to get things moving.

Once a spiritual director is able accurately to type the directee as a SP, in light of the above, it can easily be seen how differently will be the approach to direction for the SP from that of either the NF or SJ. Unfortunately, a great deal of the energy of the SPs never becomes available to the Church because of our failure to understand and provide for the needs of the SP. Although few SPs ever become spiritual directors, they should be encouraged to do so, since it often takes a SP to understand the "carpe-diem attitude" of other SPs. St. Francis of Assisi is a very typical SP, therefore every spiritual director is urged to read a good biography of St. Francis in order to discern how best to help and direct SPs. In the Gospels St. Peter is a typical SP, and St. Mark's Gospel with its emphasis on the actions of Jesus is the SP Gospel.

A SP loves a challenge, loves to be told something is difficult or even impossible. A study of how Jesus guided St. Peter may give some ideas for the spiritual direction of a SP. In the Gospels, probably the rich young man who came running up to Jesus, asking, "What must I do to be saved?" (Acts 16:30) was a SP. So the challenge that Jesus gave the rich young man to go, sell all that you possess, and give to the poor, was the right kind of direction to give a SP. Like the young man in the Gospel, not every SP will respond positively to the challenge, but if they are to be won over for God and Jesus Christ, this is the proper approach.

The SP does not need as much time alone with God in prayer as do the other three temperaments. They need perhaps twenty minutes a day for reading and reflecting on the Gospels or other biblical stories filled with action, for example, the stories of David, Moses, Elijah, Joseph of Egypt, and Paul of Tarsus. Acts of loving service can be the most effective form of prayer for the SP. If a SP has made a previous commitment to center his or her life in God and doing God's Will, all of one's external activity will be accompanied by a free-flowing, spontaneous, informal loving and praising dialogue with God. The life of St. Francis of Assisi and Franciscan spirituality give many examples of this type of prayer, for example Francis's Canticle of the Sun. Franciscan spirituality sees the beauty, goodness, and love of God everywhere and finds great joy in praising this God.

SP prayer makes full use of the five senses and is totally open to the presence of God in the whole of creation. A SP can make a prayerful meditation on the beauty of a flower, a lake, a meadow, a mountain, a waterfall, the ocean, or any event of nature such as a sunrise or sunset, a snowfall, or the changes of the seasons. When reflecting on the life of Jesus, the actions of Jesus such as his miracles will appeal especially to a SP. The parables also appeal to the SP with their unusual endings. A prayerful SP will find the thought of God predominating every waking moment. The Jesus prayer or other ejaculatory prayers are helpful to keep God constantly present in the life of the SP. They usually dislike formal, set prayers and prefer spontaneous, free-flowing dialogue with God. The SP will find very stifling to one's union with God any strict routine of prayer such as the Spiritual Exercises of St. Ignatius. To impose such a regime on a SP will usually do more harm than good. During a silent retreat the director is advised to give great freedom to the SP to follow whatever direction the Holy Spirit might lead. A daily sharing of the SP's experiences of the day with the director is recommended.

The director should always look for some challenge that God is asking of the SP at this moment of his or her life.

The SP is best at short-range projects. They need to see quick or instant results. Seeing is believing for the SP. St. Thomas the doubting apostle was probably an SP. The director needs to suggest spiritual exercises that will show some fruit in a short time rather than long-term projects. The project may be quite difficult, for example, a total fast from everything except water, for one, two, or three days will be appropriate to a healthy SP. Large sacrifices of one's time, money, and energy to do some charitable service for another will appeal to the SP and be productive of much spiritual fruit and growth. The SP thrives on the visible, audible, and tangible. They love to give gifts and see the reaction of pleasure and surprise on the face of the receiver. They love to work with their hands to produce a thing of beauty and then generously bestow their gift on another. They love to sing, play music, celebrate, have a party. In the Prayer Suggestions of chapter 6 in *Prayer and Temperament,* some suggestions are made as to how this can be made into a SP prayer.

Because of their impetuosity and generosity, SPs are fond of the "grand gesture" whereby one dramatically expresses one's commitment to God. There are many examples of these dramatic, impulsive actions in the life of St. Francis of Assisi. The SP does not respond well to the abstract or purely intellectual, but is primarily interested in the real and literal. A SP is capable of heroic sacrifices for a worthy cause. Their generosity may lead to acts of love that other temperaments would be unable to endure. Once convinced of the value of a goal, its pursuit becomes mere play and not work for the SP. The SP is willing to give up all ties to the present world in pursuit of some ideal. The spiritual director needs the wisdom to know when to encourage these heroic sacrifices and when to limit them. This will occur if both director and directee are humbly open to the Holy Spirit.

The NT (Thomistic, Promethean, Phlegmatic) Temperament

According to David Keirsey about 12 percent of the American population belongs to this temperament. Probably about an equal percentage of regular churchgoers is NT. A NT is not apt to seek spiritual direction until one has become thoroughly convinced that the only worthwhile goal in life is sanctity. This conviction may result from some deep, faith experience whereby God has touched the soul of the NT or through an intellectual conviction from reading or hearing a sermon or lecture. It can also come about from an NT meeting a very mature, balanced person who is honestly pursuing the goal of sanctity. St. John the Apostle is a NT who was converted from meeting Jesus. St. Teresa of Avila is a NT who received a special call of grace from God. St. Thomas Aquinas chose holiness of life primarily as a result of his study of God. NTs tend to be perfectionists and once they are convinced that sanctity is the highest and best perfection, they will leave no stone unturned to attain it.

NTs have a great thirst for truth and knowledge. They have a tremendous desire to understand, comprehend, explain, and predict everything. Besides a pure love of the truth, there is hidden in this desire for knowledge a secret or not so secret desire to control the environment. NTs like to control both themselves and others and frequently become leaders in whatever field they choose to follow. This drive for power, unless controlled, can dominate their whole life so that everything, including all human relationships, takes a second place. The spiritual director of a NT will need to take special pains, first of all, to make the NT aware of this inner drive and then to learn how to bring it into balance with all the other values in life. The drive must not be repressed or destroyed, but a legitimate outlet for it needs to be found. Holiness of life is one such legitimate outlet.

NTs tend to be impersonal in their pursuit of truth and power. Without realizing it, they often treat other persons as things or pawns on a chessboard instead of human beings. The NT is usually hard on one's self and very self-critical and then shows the same critical attitude toward others. Most of the spiritual direction of a NT will be spent helping one to become more personal in all the human relationships in life, starting with those with whom one lives and works. If the NT succeeds in activating his or her feeling function and gives it equal status with the thinking function, the power of the NT to do good and work wonders in the world becomes almost unlimited. Tolerance, patience, gentleness, tenderness, and long-suffering are some of the qualities of love that the director needs to insist the NT begin to practice in daily life. The NT needs to show tolerance and patience with oneself as well as others, acknowledging and admitting one's own limitations, weaknesses, faults, and failures.

Like the SP, the NT also likes challenges, especially intellectual challenges. The NT likes anything involving strategy, long-range planning. Unlike the SP, the NT is able to pursue a long-range goal that may require years or a lifetime to accomplish. They are never satisfied with the second best but want always the highest possible perfection. The spiritual director can satisfy this striving for perfection by directing the NT into the reading of the spiritual classics such as the works of St. Teresa of Avila, St. Catherine of Siena, Julian of Norwich, Meister Eckhart, and other mystical writers.

The prayer life of the NT tends to be a logical, orderly progression of thought from one point to the next until an intellectual conviction regarding the topic considered is attained. There is a real danger that this prayer degenerates into a merely scholarly research and study that remains strictly cerebral without ever reaching the heart or changing the pattern of one's life. The task of the spiritual director is to make sure that this does not happen. A recommended way to prevent this is to insist that all four steps of *Lectio Divina* be practiced in every period of prayer. Besides the meditative activity of the mind, the feelings of the heart need to be activated during the *Oratio* portion of the prayer. This in turn should lead to a *metanoia,* a real change of direction in one's whole life.

The NT often shows a great interest and fascination for contemplative prayer. The grace of passive contemplation is a gift from God and not something one can attain by mere human efforts. However, St. Teresa of Avila and other spiritual masters insist that God is ready to give this grace to anyone who properly disposes oneself for it. Knowing this, a NT who has chosen sanctity as one's main goal in life will leave no stone unturned to dispose his or her soul for the gift of passive contemplation in prayer. The spiritual director can be a great help to the NT in bringing about the proper disposition of heart for contemplative prayer. This disposition is essentially love. Love does not come easy for a NT. However, with the strong inner drive for perfection that is usually present in the NT, once a decision is made to grow in love, the spiritual direction of the NT will usually be successful.

The spiritual direction of NTs can be very satisfying to the director since one is dealing with persons who are the movers and shakers of the world. If the director can be the catalyst that brings about a deep conversion of a NT to God and holiness, then many hundreds or thousands of other persons will also be helped to grow in holiness. However, directing a NT is probably the most difficult of all the four temperaments. NTs expect perfection in their directors just as they do in themselves and in everyone else. The director of a NT especially needs to be well versed in the whole science and art of spiritual direction.

CHAPTER 14

Spiritual Direction for Contemplative Souls

Most of what is contained in this book is applicable to contemplative souls and mystics. It has been my experience that contemplatives and mystics still have clay feet. They have to struggle with the three "Ps" of possessions, pleasure, and power. God takes great delight in showering mystical and contemplative graces on souls still laboring in second and third levels of faith. It is another instance of the divine humor that St. Paul mentions in First Corinthians: "God chose what is foolish in the world to shame the wise; God chose what is weak in the world to shame the strong; God chose what is low and despised in the world, things that are not, to reduce to nothing things that are, so that no one might boast in the presence of God" (1 Cor 1:27–29).

If the spiritual director is personally experienced in contemplative prayer, there should be no problem in directing contemplative souls. However, there is a real problem if the director has no personal experience of contemplative prayer. The problem is not insoluble. St. Teresa of Avila once stated that she would prefer a learned theologian as her director rather than an unlearned saint. She was speaking from personal experience of having suffered much agony at the hands of spiritual directors who were unlearned.

There is adequate literature available to instruct spiritual directors how to help those called to contemplative prayer. Anyone wishing to become a good spiritual director should be familiar with the writings of such authors as Thomas Merton, Thomas Green, Basil Pennington, Thomas Keating, Teresa of Avila, St. John of the Cross, Francis de Sales, William McNamara, George Maloney, and William Shannon. The classic book to introduce both director and directee to contemplative prayer is *The Cloud of Unknowing*, written by an unknown author in the fourteenth century. The book that has helped me most to understand contemplative prayer and the direction of contemplative souls is *The Degrees of the Spiritual Life* by Abbe Auguste Saudreau. It is a two-volume work that is long out of print but may be found in religious libraries. I have found the books written by Thomas Green very helpful in understanding the dark night of the soul. The classic on this subject is the *Dark Night of the Soul* by St. John of the Cross. St. Teresa of Avila's book *Interior Castle* describes the different forms of contemplative prayer for better understanding. The writings by Thomas Merton in *Contemplative Prayer* are very helpful for those called to contemplative prayer.

The classic book for understanding mysticism is *Mysticism: The Nature and Development of Spiritual Consciousness* by Evelyn Underhill. The second half of her book is especially good where she gives examples from writings of mystics from different periods of history. A modern-day mystic, Bernadette Roberts, has written three books that are helpful for directing mystics and contemplatives. The titles of her books are: *The Path to No-Self: Life at the Center, The Experience of No-Self: A Contemplative Journey,* and *What Is Self?: A Study of the Spiritual Journey in Terms of Consciousness.* Another landmark book on mysticism is *Treatise on the Love of God* by St.

Francis de Sales. The book that has helped me most to understand mysticism is *The Story of a Soul,* the autobiography of St. Thérèse of Lisieux.

Contemplative Prayer

Contemplation is a form of prayer that is beyond words. It is a direct experience of God or one of God's attributes. It should be the normal result of any valid form of prayer. In *Lectio Divina* it is the fourth step that should naturally follow *Lectio, Meditatio,* and *Oratio.* It is the fourth R of *Resting* that should result from a good experience of *Reading, Reflecting,* and *Responding.* Contemplation should be the regular, natural experience of every good period of prayer. Unfortunately, most people today think of contemplative prayer as a mystical experience reserved for very holy souls at the sixth or seventh levels of faith.

Awe, wonderment, admiration are some of the words that help us understand what is meant by contemplative prayer. We have an experience of contemplation every time we find ourselves overwhelmed by God's goodness, love, mercy, forgiveness, gentleness, patience, loving care, tolerance, generosity, justice, humility, persistence, and sense of humor. Whenever we are aware of any of these transcendental traits of God, we have had an experience of contemplative prayer. Anytime we feel overwhelmed with gratitude to God for some blessing received, we are thereby experiencing contemplation. All of these experiences take us beyond words to a direct experience of God. During contemplation we are aware that there are no adequate words to explain our experience.

The spiritual direction for contemplative prayer is to encourage everyone to welcome these moments of awe and wonderment regarding God that we experience. This is a higher form of prayer than meditation or vocal prayer. Anytime we experience the presence of God or one of his infinite traits, we will be at a loss for words to adequately describe the experience. However, words are not necessary while contemplating God.

Because they cannot find words to describe their experience of God, many people imagine that this experience is not prayer. If we make a serious effort to practice the first three steps of *Lectio Divina,* this contemplation of God should be the result. We do not have to be totally awestruck or overwhelmed to have contemplative prayer. We need simply to gaze in awe and wonderment at one or other attribute of God and God's presence in our life. Contemplation may be a simple resting in God's loving care. Contemplation often happens while taking a walk or viewing a sunset or a lake or listening to some inspiring music.

The seven gifts of the Holy Spirit lead to contemplation. Fear of the Lord overwhelms us with the greatness of God. Piety gives us an experience of intimacy with God. Counsel reveals God's Will to us. Fortitude gives us the strength to do God's Will. Knowledge helps us see the hand of God's loving care at work in the events of our life. Understanding helps us to better understand the mysteries of God. Wisdom gives us an experience of God's presence similar to heaven. If we make ourselves open to any one of the gifts of the Holy Spirit, we will have an experience of contemplation. The fruits of the Holy Spirit are some of the names we give to this experience: love, joy, peace, patience, kindness, goodness, generosity, gentleness, tolerance, self-control, faithfulness, purity, balance, and moderation.

Dark Night

There are two ways to define *dark night*. In a general way it is the experience of the cross in our life. It may be defined as anything that happens to us that is contrary to the way we would want it to happen. It is what Pierre Teilhard de Chardin calls our diminishments in *The Divine Milieu*. A second way to define *dark night* is the dryness, coldness, and lack of feeling of the presence of God that we frequently experience in prayer. This is the meaning of *dark night of the soul* in the writings of St. John of the Cross. St. John of the Cross also writes about the *dark night of the senses,* which is the loss of all pleasures of the senses. It is during these dark nights that a person needs the help of a spiritual director more than any other time. During these dark nights a person is not capable of making good decisions regarding oneself and therefore needs to depend on the judgment of a wise, experienced counselor.

We bring upon ourselves some of our dark nights by our selfishness, pride, foolishness, neglect of self-discipline, and overindulgence in one or more of the three "Ps": possessions, pleasure, and power, Many dark nights happen to us without our being in any way responsible. They may be due to the faults, mistakes, ignorance of others, or simply the normal events of our life on Earth. Still other dark nights are due to the special grace of God who intervenes in our life in order to lead us to a higher level of faith and union with God. There is need of a dark night of the senses in order to wean us away from second level of faith to third level and from third level to fourth level. There is need of a dark night of the soul in order to help us graduate from fourth to fifth levels of faith and again from the fifth to sixth levels. The purpose of the dark night of the senses is to bring about a total detachment from sensual pleasure. The purpose of the dark night of the soul is to wean us away from the former basis for belief and establish a more solid basis for faith. The experience of dark night enables us to center our life totally in God and away from self and thus accomplish a union of love with God. Frequently the dark night of the soul will last for many years. In the case of Teresa of Avila it lasted more than eighteen years. "We know that all things work together for good for those who love God, who are called according to his purpose" (Rom 8:28).

Some examples of dark nights people may experience are:

1. Dryness, distractions in prayer, unable to concentrate on God;
2. Discouragement, loss of hope and meaning, no will or desire to live;
3. Loneliness, absence of friends and love, inability to love others;
4. Fear, anxiety, insecurity, uncertainty of the future;
5. Lack of enthusiasm, lack of physical or emotional energy;
6. Severe temptations of faith, sex, anger, resentment, hatred;
7. Mental confusion, mental illness, serious or chronic physical illness;
8. Failure of marriage, parenting, divorce, marital problems;
9. Failure at work, loss of job, unhappiness at work, unable to find job;
10. Financial difficulties, lack of sufficient money, unable to pay debts;
11. Stress, burnout, tension, exhaustion, chronic tiredness;
12. Absence of worthwhile goals in life, meaningless existence;
13. Addictions, mistakes, faults, sins of past and present;
14. Absence of spiritual progress, regression to former faults, failures;
15. Persecution, opposition from others, envy and hatred of others;
16. Retirement, old age, terminal illness, presence of death.

Spiritual Direction for Those Suffering a Dark Night

It is not advisable for a person suffering a dark night to try to discern the origin of the problem alone, but only with the help of a trusted friend or counselor. We are not capable of making good judgments if we are experiencing desolation. If possible, it is better to wait until we have found true peace of soul before investigating the cause. During the dark night one should live in the present moment and learn how best to survive this experience of the cross. The spiritual director will encourage the sufferer to hold on to faith, hope, and love. By faith we become totally convinced that God is all-wise, all-good, all-powerful, all-loving, and always faithful to his word and promises. (Faith is a way of seeing in the dark.) By hope we learn to trust ourselves blindly and totally into the hands of God's loving care. (Hope is a way of possessing what is beyond our reach.) By love we choose to center our life in God and the doing of God's Will rather than our own will. (Charity is a way of loving God purely and above all else.) The two basic attitudes needed to handle our dark nights are detachment and total trust in God's loving care. We strive to be detached from all desires on our part and completely open to go in any direction God seems to be leading us. We try to convince ourselves that God is able to bring good out of everything, even the darkest night (Rom 8:28).

It is important that the directee not change or abandon one's prayer time during a dark night, even if it seems a total waste of time. One of the purposes of every dark night is to teach us to love and serve the God of consolation rather than the consolations of God. One should continue to give the same amount of time to prayer as was customary at other times. Even if constantly distracted, the directee is advised calmly to redirect one's attention to God and the desire to do God's Will each time one becomes aware of the distraction. This requires an act of the will that is very pleasing to God. It is pure faith, hope, and charity. "I believe; help my unbelief!" (Mark 9:24).

Dark nights require a humble acceptance of the mystery of God and the mystery of evil and suffering. There is so much we do not understand. We grow in humility and authenticity by a blind, humble acceptance of God's Will along with a conviction that God can and will bring good even out of evil. We must learn to let go and let God handle the outcome of our suffering. The constant teaching of Jesus in the Gospels is that God is ever willing to forgive us and will never abandon us, regardless of the situation.

It is advisable that a person suffering a dark night should try to be especially generous in charity and almsgiving to others who are more unfortunate than oneself. Since even the darkest night of suffering is unable to take away our desires, one is advised at such times to have immense desires for all the transcendentals: love, justice, truth, peace, goodness, beauty, unity. Use whatever power of will one has to desire to center one's life in God and the doing of God's Will. An essential part of the desire for God and God's Will is the willingness to be totally detached from every other desire except God's Will. St. John of the Cross states that it makes no difference whether a bird is tied down to Earth by a heavy rope or a single thread; it is unable to fly away until it has broken that one little thread. All our dark nights have as their purpose to break the many threads of attachment that now tie us down to Earth.

We are able to prepare ourselves spiritually and psychologically for these dark nights so that when they occur, we are better able to handle them. We do this by growing in humility, faith, hope, love, self-discipline, and detachment during times of peace and consolation. Jesus says that there are certain kinds of evil spirits that are cast out only by prayer and fasting (Matt

17:21). Best of all we prepare ourselves by the practice of total obedience to the Will of God as it is revealed to us through our conscience and our prayer.

Father Thomas Green says our relationship with God is similar to that of a marriage and has three stages: courtship, honeymoon, and marriage. The courtship between God and ourselves has a dual purpose of knowledge of God and knowledge of ourselves. This is the time to use those five methods of prayer and meditation described in *Prayer and Temperament*. This may go on for many years but the time comes when we can have first-hand experiences of God's love for us and our love for God without the need of words. This is the honeymoon. We usually have such experiences from time to time during our life on Earth. It is whenever our relationship with God moves from the head to the heart, from second step of *Lectio Divina* to third step. We experience great joy in being with the God who loves us and whom we love very, very much. We have spontaneous prayers of love, joy, consolation, and peace. We love simply to be present in love to God and God to us. But the honeymoon usually comes to an end and the long, hard work of establishing a permanent marriage with God begins. This is when the dark nights begin to appear, perhaps first as alternating periods of desolation. It is during this third stage that we gradually learn to let go of self-love and self-seeking and become totally centered in God. We learn to love God for his sake and not for our sake. Gradually our only concern is what will make God most happy with no concern for ourselves. All the dark nights in our life have as their purpose this ultimate union with God. However, it is especially the dark night between fifth and sixth levels of faith that accomplishes this. St. John of the Cross says that few souls reach this point but all souls are called to it.

St. John of the Cross gives three signs to test the authenticity of the dark night of the soul as being from God and not our fault. (1) We find no consolation either in God, the things of God or in anything created. We are no longer attracted to the pleasures of this world. (2) Our memory is centered on God and our one desire is the doing of God's Will but this is done with painful care and solicitude. We are miserable when with God but even more miserable without him. "I cannot find God yet desperately need to find him." (3) One is no longer able to use the four steps of *Lectio Divina* in prayer as formerly. We look back with longing to the times when we were able to pray and meditate. Father Thomas Green gives a fourth sign of the authenticity of this dark night of the soul. (4) One is willing to live with this darkness and accept it peacefully, provided one can believe that it is God working in us to purify our love for him. One feels great fear of losing the God whom one loves so much. (See p. 119 of *When the Well Runs Dry: Prayer beyond the Beginnings* by Thomas Green. See also his book, *Drinking from a Dry Well.*) Another reference for understanding the dark night of the soul: St. John of the Cross, *Dark Night of the Soul,* Book I, chapters 8, 9, 10.

We must never try to force things during the dark night. There is always a subtle self-love mixed with our noblest actions and aspirations. We need the two dark nights in order to purge ourselves of this self-love. They allow us to experience our own nothingness and sinfulness. As a result we stop taking ourselves too seriously. We become at peace with this self-knowledge when we realize that God loves us as we are, sins and all. We come to peaceful terms with reality of who God is and who we are. This is the truth that will set us free (John 8:32). By the dark nights we are purified of every attachment except our attachment to God and God's Will. The darkness we experience is actually the presence of the blinding light of God's truth.

Active and Passive Dark Nights

Both the dark night of senses and dark night of soul have an active and a passive phase. The active phase is where we do all in our power to cooperate with God's grace to bring about the total detachment from self and attachment to God. The passive phase is where God takes over the work of detachment and we simply allow this to happen. The active phase of the dark night of senses usually occurs during second and third levels of faith. The passive phase of dark night of senses usually occurs between the third and fourth levels of faith. The active phase of dark night of soul occurs throughout the fourth and fifth levels of faith. The passive phase of dark night of soul usually occurs between fifth and sixth levels. This passive phase may continue for many years.

The Mystery of Suffering

In one way or another, sooner or later, everyone is given a taste of the bitter cup of suffering. Jesus spoke of this in the Gospels when he asked James and John if they were willing to drink of the cup of the passion. Some are given a greater share of this suffering, some less. At present we do not understand the mystery of how and why God distributes suffering in such a varied degree among different persons. Believing firmly that God's Will is always right and good, we must simply make an act of blind faith and trust in his decisions and providence.

In some mysterious way, all suffering, whether Jesus' or our own, contributes in a positive way to the conquering of evil in the world and to the salvation of the human race. Many theories have been proposed as to why and how Jesus' suffering and our suffering neutralize and overcome evil and sin. It still remains a mystery. Perhaps at some future date God will reveal more clearly the mystery of suffering. For the present we must bow to Job's decision that is given at the end of forty chapters of struggling with it: "Therefore I have uttered what I did not understand, things too wonderful for me, which I did not know" (Job 42:3). St. Paul gives this response: "We proclaim Christ crucified, a stumbling-block to Jews and foolishness to Gentiles, but to those who are the called, both Jews and Greeks, Christ the power of God and the wisdom of God." (1 Cor 1:23–34).

CHAPTER 15

A Balanced Christianity

St. Thomas Aquinas says that virtue stands in the middle between two opposing extremes. Balance between opposite poles runs as a constant theme throughout the whole of authentic Christianity. This balance is the opposite of extremism or fanaticism that takes only one aspect of truth and exaggerates it while other opposing aspects are ignored. Heresy results by taking a particular insight while denying another equally true aspect of religion.

Many Christians find satisfaction in accusing those who disagree with them of being fanatics but fail to recognize the seeds of fanaticism in their own stubbornly held position. All of us, in one way or another, at one time in our life or another, are fanatical about something. This seems to be the lot of human existence on Earth and a part of the original sin we have inherited from our ancestors. We are somewhat like drunk drivers who are never able to keep a straight line but wander from one side to another. It behooves us to recognize and accept ownership for our own particular brand of extremism. Because of the tension that a balance demands, with the constant struggle necessary to maintain it, countless Christians have sought to eliminate certain of their problems by denying one or the other opposing pole. This only gives a temporary relief; the problem simply erupts at some later date.

Christianity is based on a conjunction of opposites: namely, the divine versus the human nature of Jesus Christ. The more we seek the perfection that makes us Christ-like, the harder we must strive to bring all our energies or powers into a balance between indulgence and austerity. In fact, all of our life we will be working to bring into a balance all those opposites within our nature. The opposites should maintain their individuality and at the same time be in conjunction with each other. Examples of such counterparts are: happiness/suffering, attachment/detachment, self-development/renunciation, self-indulgence/self-denial, body/spirit, activity/passivity, intellect/feeling, introversion/extraversion, positive/negative, male/female, and life/death. The Book of Ecclesiastes (3:1–6) states this need for balance very poetically: "For everything there is a season, and a time for every matter under heaven…a time to seek, and a time to lose; a time to keep, and a time to throw away…"

Balance between Self-Development and Renunciation

Self-development and renunciation—self-expression and self-denial—are not mutually exclusive but part of the general rhythm of growth from a lower to higher level of maturity. They are like the breathing-in and breathing-out of our body: two components of a healthy, developing life but subject to an infinite number of subtle variations. The exact blending calls for spiritual tact and wisdom that needs to be improved constantly. It is quite difficult to strike a proper harmony. We need a very high tension capacity to live under the strain necessary for growth. Because self-discipline will increase our tension capacity, we need especially to emphasize self-denial. Those who lead an easy and comfortable existence often lack the will power and strength to live under heavy strain. The fullest development of our potential occurs only when we willingly undergo pain and suffering, either by way of self-discipline or through the external circumstances in which we live.

However, in our self-denial we must take care not to destroy or break our ego completely. It is vital that we maintain a certain tension and balance between a strong ego and a strong self-discipline. Both are important and both are needed for growth in perfection and maturity. (A total loss of ego-strength would result in the powerful forces of our unconscious flooding into our conscious life and would bring about a breakdown of our psyche and result in a real psychosis.) We need not be discouraged when we sometimes go to extremes in the matter of self-indulgence, for it seems that some strong personalities must suffer the humiliation of many falls in order to awaken them to reality and train them in the proper balance. No one should ever presume to commit deliberate sin; but if sin should occur, even serious sin, there need be no discouragement. We must be willing to repent and try, try, try again.

We should accept with gratitude and delight whatever pleasures and joys God's providence gives us; but let us not linger too long in the enjoyment of them. We need to keep going forward and upward to attain an ever-higher degree of love and life. We must constantly strive to bring our whole self, both inner and outer, into subjection to the higher law of the universe, which is another way of saying "God's Will." To do this we must keep a tension in our daily lives between attachment and detachment, between pleasure and pain, between struggle and rest, between activity and passivity, between self-development and renunciation. Often it is necessary to choose minimum pleasure rather than maximum pleasure. We need quite frequently to sacrifice bodily and worldly gratification to make room for the life of love to grow within us. Only by frequent restraint are we able to keep our human nature on an even keel and open to the diverse experiences needed for continued growth in wholeness.

Attachment versus Detachment

Christian asceticism does not thwart our highest, deepest, and greatest aspirations. To the contrary, our lesser and more ephemeral desires are sacrificed to make room for the higher and eternal aspirations. The road of life climbs upward and has a goal that is more spiritual than physical. Therefore, the highest possible spiritualization and the ultimate goals of life are not found in the temporal, material zones of this world but in a total transformation of ourselves into a wholeness similar to that of the risen Christ. We need to go beyond the frontiers of the visible world and frequently sacrifice the good we now possess for the sake of a total "beyond." We need to transcend our earthly selves in order to reach the higher dimension of reality we call God.

The striving for higher values is not a case of masochistically diminishing our present enjoyment of earthly life. There is a definite place and need for such pleasures. We are not meant to be cold blooded and unfeeling toward others but to feel a real attachment to loved ones: spouse, children, friends, relatives, country, and so forth. The personality becomes warped when one's whole life is filled with suffering and tragedy, just as all pleasure and no pain creates an imbalance in the opposite direction. As the Book of Ecclesiastes (3:1, 4) says, "For everything there is a season...a time to weep, and a time to laugh; a time to mourn, and a time to dance." We need discernment and wisdom to know when it is the right time for both.

Of the two, attachment and detachment, the more difficult is detachment. We all desire pleasure more than pain; therefore most of our effort should be spent in developing the art of detachment and finding satisfaction and fulfillment by this path. Self-denial does not mean repressing and destroying any of our inner powers but simply controlling them and directing them into proper channels.

There is a general tendency on the part of human nature to sloth and procrastination, especially when struggle and pain might be our lot. We must exercise our faculties of growth by sacrificing our egotistic desires every day. Thousands of such decisions are required in a lifetime. We need to break the chains of laziness, selfishness, greed, lust, and gluttony. Basically these chains, which the New Testament often symbolizes by the word *world,* promote the love of self to the exclusion of the love of God and neighbor.

There is more than a spiritual value to self-denial. Out psychological health demands it. People who live only for the satisfaction of their selfish, bodily desires are disowned not only by the rest of mankind but are also rejected by their own inner self. They find themselves plagued by frustration, irritability, guilt, tension, fear, ugly moods, and unhappiness. They are closed in themselves and become blind to the needs of others and the good of humankind as a whole. The sooner we learn the difficult art of self-discipline, and the higher we develop our ability to endure pain and tension, the more quickly we will progress to maturity. Those who choose self-indulgence and the most comfortable life bring their growth in wholeness to a halt and gradually regress into a more infantile way of life.

In his book *Man's Search for Meaning: An Introduction to Logotherapy,* Viktor Frankl tells that those in the Nazi concentration camps of World War II who lacked a dimension in life higher than mere earthly satisfaction and bodily pleasure were soon crushed and lost the will to live. The same is true for anyone who undergoes pain for prolonged periods of time without having some higher meaning in life. If we are willing to believe that life is not a total absurdity and that the world is not total chaos but has some semblance of order and plan, then our faith will lead us to the conviction that there is another dimension of life transcendent to what we see and know on Earth. In the words of Jesus: "Be on your guard against all kinds of greed; for one's life does not consist in the abundance of possessions." (Luke 12:15). To be true to our inner nature and become authentic we must make contact with the spiritual, transcendental dimensions of life and make the necessary sacrifices to attain them.

The earlier in life we come to an understanding of the value of detachment and self-denial, the more quickly we will progress toward maturity and wholeness. Ideally, we learn self-discipline during the first twenty-five years of life, when we can best and most easily train our conscious faculties of mind, will, memory, feeling, and imagination. However, if for some reason, either through ignorance or neglect, we failed to master self-control of our conscious faculties during youth, we will need to accomplish this all-important task later in life. But the later we delay the practice of detachment, the more rigorous and lengthy the regime of self-discipline we will need. After the age of thirty we find ourselves burdened with other tasks of maturity and frequently those who have had a too comfortable and easy life in youth find themselves burdened with mental, emotional, and psychological maladjustments during the middle years of their life. However, it is never too late to begin a program of self-discipline to bring about the needed integration of our inner faculties and attain a balance in our nature.

Freedom versus Submission

One of the most basic reasons for practicing self-discipline is to experience the fullness of the freedom we need in order to love. Those persons who are not self-disciplined become slaves to whatever bodily or worldly desire they find themselves excessively attached. Only free persons are capable of love, since love means to make a free choice of giving oneself and one's life to this or that person or in this or that particular direction. In order to develop our potential for love, we need to experience freedom and detachment from the enemies of love: greed, egotism, and the excessive love of bodily pleasure. These are the three basic slaveries that prevent our attainment of maturity and sanctity. They are the three basic temptations that Jesus suffered in the desert. All three temptations center in a misuse of power. To overcome them, Jesus had to submit his desires to a higher will than his own. Only by humble submission and a transformation of these baser instincts do we obtain the freedom to love God and our neighbor and ourselves in the proper proportion.

In the first temptation Jesus was urged by Satan to use the power of God for his own personal needs, namely to change stones into bread in order to satisfy his hunger. Jesus was aware that he had been given special powers and it would have been so easy to use them for his own personal benefit. It all seemed so clear. He was hungry. He had the power. Why not use it? But intuitively Jesus knew that these special gifts of the Spirit were given to carry out his God-given mission on Earth. He must never take personal advantage of God's special gifts, never personally profit from his powers. To do so would have been the beginning of enslavement to the desires and cravings of the body. The way to freedom and the way to love required his submission to the higher Will of God: "One does not live by bread alone, but by every word that comes from the mouth of God" (Matt 4:4). Only by submission to God's Will, with the necessary self-denial, do we escape from slavery to the flesh and senses.

In the second temptation Jesus was enticed to use his powers of the Spirit to establish his control over the lives and destinies of human beings similar to the way the kings of Earth are accustomed to use their powers. Why not live up to the popular Jewish expectations of the Messiah as a world ruler and establish an earthly kingdom rather than a heavenly one? "All these I will give you, if you will fall down and worship me," Satan tells him. Jesus said to him, "Away with you, Satan! for it is written, 'Worship the Lord your God, and serve only him'" (Matt 4:9–10). Jesus was given a choice of submissions: either to God or to Satan. If he misused his newly received powers in the service of greed and worldly ambition, he would be in slavery to Satan with the resulting loss of freedom. Only by denying worldly power and submitting himself to God's plan of salvation did he obtain the freedom necessary to love.

The third temptation was the suggestion to misuse his powers by taking things into his own hands rather than submitting humbly to God's plan. To show off his powers by floating down out of the sky into the temple courtyard was a temptation to pride and egotism. The alternative to this display was to take the way of the cross. The temptation was to take a short-cut to glory rather than the way of rejection, failure, dishonor, suffering, insult, agony, and death. Satan urged him: "If you are the Son of God, throw yourself down; for it is written, 'He will command his angels concerning you,' and 'On their hands they will bear you up, so that you will not dash your foot against a stone'" (Matt 4:6).

The three temptations of sensuality, greed, and pride that Jesus encountered and mastered are the three basic temptations all of us have to face. In all three instances we are dealing not with an absolute evil but rather with a divinely created instinct that has a tendency to go to extremes and become a law unto itself. Instead of keeping to their proper functions as submissive servants to the total destiny of our life, they try to become independent of all control. Sensuality is when the instinct for self-preservation and the preservation of the species (sex) bows to a base, selfish expression. Greed is the instinct for freedom and independence expressed through the selfish hoarding of worldly possessions and power to the detriment of others. Pride is the instinct of self-love reigning supreme over the duty to serve God and neighbor. In all these situations we are dealing with a great potential for good and evil that resists submitting itself to higher aspirations.

In order to keep these instincts under control we must practice self-denial, detachment, and renunciation of excesses in each of these areas. Such renunciation may mean real pain and sacrifice of something we want very much; but this is the way to redeem these God-given instincts and free ourselves from slavery to self, to pleasure, and to worldly goods. When we willingly accept the suffering involved in attaining freedom from these three forms of idolatry, we are carrying our cross. Thus the cross becomes the symbol of the effort required for our growth from slavery to freedom.

Self-denial is required to liberate the higher powers within us and to organize the proper priorities of our energies and the objects of our love. The egocentric shell that we have built around our conscious life must be broken open in order to allow the bright sunlight of God's love to flood our whole being. Each time our egotism suffers a defeat, we experience pain and frequently we imagine that we are losing something essential to our welfare. Actually, the opposite is true. Each time we give into our selfish desires for pleasure, material possessions, or worldly honors and ambitions, we become enslaved to these lesser powers and lose our freedom to practice the higher spiritual powers. Either we allow ourselves to be possessed by love, or things of this Earth will possess us. This is another way of saying that we must sacrifice everything for love, because God is love (1 John 4:8).

Fulfillment versus Diminishment

A truly balanced life will have both fulfillment and diminishment. Unless we experience the fulfillment of at least some of our goals and objectives, we will become discouraged, bitter, and pessimistic. On the other hand, a person who never experiences failure will lose sight of his or her creatureliness and will rapidly assume the posture of a god. This is always a danger to those who are given power over the lives of their fellow human beings; and those who are invested with lifetime positions of power are especially vulnerable to pride and arrogance. A mature balanced life will be a good mix of success and failure, of fulfillment and diminishment, of activity and passivity, and of death and resurrection.

For many people there is no need to look for opportunities to practice diminishment. Divine providence provides them with ample opportunities through illness, pain, and physical, material, and spiritual losses. St. Paul states: "We know that all things work together for good for those who love God, who are called according to his purpose" (Rom 8:28). If we accept these uninvited crosses with patience and love, they will help us to establish the right priorities in our life and to reach the desired goal of wholeness. However, if they are accepted with resentment, they will hinder, not advance, our progress toward maturity. This does not mean that we are not allowed to use the ordinary commonsense means to eliminate these pains and losses from our life. Rather an attitude of detachment and a proper regard for the right priorities must be cultivated. We need to realize that there are other things that are more important than the avoidance of pain and loss. For example, love is a more positive and productive power than freedom from pain. Therefore, for the sake of love, we should be willing to endure pain or loss. This is the example Jesus himself gave us in his passion and death.

The best way to find where we need to diminish our egotistic self is to discover the things to which we are excessively attached, things about which we would be upset if they were suddenly removed from our lives. Examples of such excessive attachment are: alcohol, tobacco, coffee, drugs, sex, soft drinks, clothes, TV, golf, tennis, football, and so forth. We need to study our habits and discern the things on which we spend time, money, and energy. How concerned would we become if one or the other of these enjoyments were denied us? A good way to find the answer is to deny ourselves the enjoyment of one of these things for a period of time, for example, during the six weeks of Lent, and see how we react.

Diminishment or detachment has a broader meaning than the sacrifice of pleasure and possessions. Among other things it means the ability to love others without possessing them, to respect others as free persons and not to manipulate and use them as things for the attainment of some selfish goal. Love is the primal and universal energy of life, the attraction by which parts of the whole are drawn toward one another. Its purpose is to bring about a final Unity of all within the center that is God. In order for this potential for love to develop fully and properly, we must break down the partitions that still divide us from one another and divide one part of our being from another. This is the primary purpose of all self-denial and diminishment. Its goal is the oneness with God for which Jesus prayed the night before he died. It is the unity which St. Paul says will occur at the end of time: "When all things are subjected to him, then the Son himself will also be subjected to the one who put all things in subjection under him, so that God may be all in all" (1 Cor 15:28).

The inner direction of our heart is influenced by all the selfish decisions in our life. Past wrong decisions make us weak and vacillating in the present. A history of past selfishness requires many years of self-denial and acceptance of uninvited crosses of diminishment to change the direction of our heart from self toward God and love. Even after forgiveness, the evil effects of past excesses continue for a long time, even past our death into the lives of those who come after us. However, we must not be pessimistic about ourselves and our possibilities of success. Instead, we must bravely face each new challenge, regardless of how often we may fail. There can be no permanent tragedy if, with humble confidence in the power of God, we keep trying.

Death versus Resurrection

The paschal mystery of death and resurrection runs through the whole mystery of life. Jesus tells us, "Very truly, I tell you, unless a grain of wheat falls into the earth and dies, it remains just a single grain; but if it dies, it bears much fruit" (John 12:24). Again and again in his Epistles, St. Paul insists that every Christian must experience this paschal mystery—that we must die to this world in order to rise to God's world. "Therefore we have been buried with him by baptism into death, so that, just as Christ was raised from the dead by the glory of the Father, so we too might walk in newness of life. For if we have been united with him in a death like his, we will certainly be united with him in a resurrection like his" (Rom 6:4–5).

The cross is the symbol of the asceticism required to rise above our nature and reach participation in the higher nature of God. Our Christian faith assures us that we have been called to share God's life. To participate in this divine life some of our present ways must die and we must rise to a more Christ-like way of life. By sacrificing the externals of life, we allow the more important inner powers to take root and grow. The present is sacrificed in order that it may be transcended and a new life developed. Rather than selfishly clinging to our present, we must empty ourselves of this present, sacrifice the old, and allow the new to be born. Over and over again we must disengage ourselves and go beyond to something higher. This requires detachment, poverty of spirit, and willingness to sacrifice. Somehow we must overcome our fear and find the courage to crucify our egotism. Each time our egotism suffers a defeat, we experience pain; but this pain becomes a loving fire that completes our union with God. To live the paschal mystery we must be ready to suffer the loss of many things that worldly people consider essential.

To put our faith in the paschal mystery as the ultimate solution to the problems of life means to accept the presence of unresolved tragedy. To accept and live the paschal mystery means an acceptance of suffering and death that are not resolved in this present life, but only in some mysterious way in the life beyond the grave. We call this resolution *resurrection*. We don't really know what the New Testament means by the actual process of resurrection, because it is a life quite different from all our present experiences; but once we put our faith in it, we can live with the possibility of incompleteness, rather than success, as the end of earthly life. Hence the all-importance of the resurrection of Jesus for a balanced Christianity. As St. Paul says: "If there is no resurrection of the dead, then Christ has not been raised; and if Christ has not been raised, then our proclamation has been in vain and your faith has been in vain....If Christ has not been raised, your faith is futile and you are still in your sins. Then those also who have died in Christ have perished. If for this life only we have hoped in Christ, we are of all people most to be pitied. But in fact Christ has been raised from the dead, the first fruits of those who have died....[F]or as all die in Adam, so all will be made alive in Christ" (1 Cor 15:13–22).

CHAPTER 16

Pitfalls in Spiritual Direction

There is an old proverb that says, "forewarned is forearmed." The purpose of this chapter is to forewarn both directors and directees of some of the dangers that need to be avoided in spiritual direction. When they occur they can endanger the success of direction. The director must never forget that God is the primary spiritual director of every soul. The human director is merely a catalyst or a midwife assisting in bringing to birth the life of God in the directee. John the Baptist is a good model for all spiritual directors. One might think of those pictures of John as always pointing to Jesus and saying, "Here is the Lamb of God who takes away the sin of the world!" (John 1:29). John's disciples complained to John that Jesus was baptizing farther up the river and all were flocking to Jesus. John's reply was, "No one can receive anything except what has been given from heaven. You yourselves are my witnesses that I said, 'I am not the Messiah, but I have been sent ahead of him.' He who has the bride is the bridegroom. The friend of the bridegroom, who stands and hears him, rejoices greatly at the bridegroom's voice. For this reason my joy has been fulfilled. He must increase, but I must decrease" (John 3:27–30).

The task of the director is, like John the Baptist, to lead people to Christ, while staying in the background. The important thing is the relationship between God and the directee. The director must be careful never to come between these two. The director must "let go, let God." The director must never try to play God by allowing ego inflation to take over and try to attract the directee to oneself rather than to God. Because spiritual direction is a counseling experience, directors run the same risk as do all counselors, namely transference. This risk is especially present when director and directee are of different sex. Since direction frequently deals with very intimate details of one's life, there is a tendency for the directee to project unconsciously on the director the archetype that Jung calls animus or anima. Likewise, unless the director is mature and knowledgeable of this phenomenon of transference, the director has a similar tendency to project his or her anima/animus on the directee. When this happens, we have a case of "falling in love" between director and directee.

The transference can be either positive or negative. The positive is present when director or directee or both transfer or project on the other the positive qualities of the unconscious anima/animus archetype and this is the more dangerous. The negative is present when one projects the negative qualities of anima/animus on the other. Such a negative transference frequently results in the end of the relationship between the two of them, unless the director is mature enough to handle this.

Carl Jung insists that there will always be some sort of transference in every counseling experience. It is most dangerous when the transference is unconscious. Therefore, the director needs to be fully aware of this problem and take the necessary measures to prevent harm to the directee. If the projection is strong, the directee needs to be told and warned. It is quite possible that the attraction or repulsion between the two of them is so strong that the best thing to do is to bring to an end the spiritual direction and recommend another spiritual director.

In addition to the sexual archetypes of anima/animus, there is also the tendency for directees to project or transfer other unconscious archetypes on the director. Examples of these are father, mother, lord, doctor, priest, king, friend, and enemy. It is the responsibility of the director to have an awareness of this phenomenon of unconscious projection. Then one can take the needed steps to avoid harm arising from it. Harm will usually be avoided if the director is mature and has most of his or her needs for giving and receiving love fulfilled in some other way outside of spiritual direction. When this is true, the director is able openly and dispassionately to discuss the problem with the directee and point out what needs to be done to avoid harm to either person or perhaps to a third party, the spouse of either the director or directee.

In order to forestall the beginning of transference the director must be constantly aware of his or her role as a catalyst who stays as much as possible in the background and, like John the Baptist, constantly points the directee toward God and Jesus Christ. However, if the director is insecure or has a poor self-image or is lacking good experiences of love in life, transference and projection will be a dangerous pitfall. There is a tendency, especially if the director is male, to exert one's power-drive and to find satisfaction in having the directee completely submissive to the director. Also, if the director is a person who is insecure or lonely, he or she will have the desire to have as many deep relationships of love with the directees as is possible. This of course is a serious abuse of the whole science of spiritual direction.

Another pitfall to be avoided is the tendency of some directors to demand blind obedience from directee to every suggestion of director. A similar desire to give blind obedience to the director is present in directees who feel incapable of making decisions for themselves. This is the problem of directive versus nondirective counseling. If the director is totally nondirective, the only value will be that the directee has the opportunity to verbalize one's spiritual problems. The director needs to be directive but not too directive. A good balance needs to be kept between both extremes. Ultimately the directee should follow one's own common sense and make one's own decisions. The suggestions of the director are to help the directee make a good decision as to which way to go. The only exception to this is when the directee is overscrupulous and is unable to make a decision as to what is sinful and not sinful. The only remedy for this spiritual disease is blind obedience to the director.

Because so much good results from spiritual direction, there is always present the pitfall of pride for the director. One imagines that it is due to one's own efforts as a director that has enabled the directee to progress spiritually. Therefore, the director must practice humility by giving total credit to God for the graces received. As St. Paul says, "What do you have that you did not receive? And if you received it, why do you boast as if it were not a gift?" (1 Cor 4:7) Also, the director must be ready to admit when one does not know the answer to a question or problem presented by the directee. By humbly admitting, "I don't know what you should do," the credibility of the director is thereby enhanced. The director should be humble and wise enough to advise a directee to go elsewhere for direction when the director feels unable to help the directee.

Another pitfall to be avoided by the director is to feel too great a concern for the feelings of the directee so that the director is silent about some fault that needs to be discussed. Accountability to another human being is probably the single greatest value in spiritual direction. This accountability will only succeed when the director feels free to talk about obvious faults of the directee that need to be corrected.

Another pitfall for the director is to try to put every directee in the same mold and treat everyone exactly the same.

This tendency may show itself when the director has experienced an important grace in his or her own journey of faith. Now the director imagines that every other person will benefit exactly the same way as did the director. Every soul is different and God leads each soul on a unique spiritual journey. It is the task of the director to try to discern what is the particular way that God is leading each soul that comes for direction and then to follow that path instead of some preconceived ideas of the director.

A real problem arises when the directee is at a higher level of faith than the director. Unless the director is quite wise as well as well versed and learned in the higher levels of faith, there will be the tendency to hold the directee back and try to make the directee conform to the things that are appropriate for the level of faith of the director. It is still possible for a director to give good direction to a soul who is at a higher level of faith than the director. For this to happen the director needs to be thoroughly familiar with what the spiritual masters have written regarding direction for these higher mansions. However, if there is some other director more capable of directing the person, it would be wise to recommend the directee to go to that person. There is no substitute for the actual experience of each of the levels of faith.

The directee must be careful not to have too high expectations of what the director can do to help one on the journey of faith. Sometimes the directee expects the humanly impossible of the director. The value of spiritual direction is great but it is still limited. Similarly, a director must be careful not to expect too much too quickly of a directee. There is a certain natural rhythm of spiritual growth that is somewhat similar to the rhythms of physical and psychological growth. If a soul is forced to grow too quickly into holiness and wholeness, the results will be artificial and not authentic.

It has been said that the best director is the least director. By this is meant that the director must not interfere too directly in the intimate relationship that is supposed to exist between each soul and God. The director must stay on the sidelines, always there as a spiritual friend to help the directee, but must never come between the directee and God. The director should endeavor to measure up to all the qualities recommended in chapter 4 as the ideal qualities of a good spiritual director. The director should then encourage each directee gradually to progress from one level of faith to the next and thus live out all those qualities of the directee recommended in chapter 5.

CHAPTER 17

How to Deal with Extraordinary Spiritual Phenomena

Before very long almost every spiritual director will be forced to deal with a directee who claims to have had some sort of extraordinary spiritual experience. It may be a vision of some sort or what is called a *locution,* in other words, a voice of God or Blessed Mother or some other supernatural being that speaks to them. My own experience of giving spiritual direction for more than fifty years is that approximately one in every five persons that comes for spiritual direction will have a problem whether to accept such phenomena as truly from God.

There are two extremes that must be avoided by the spiritual director in handling such claims. It is a mistake to be too gullible in accepting at face value every claim a directee has regarding such visions or locutions. It is also a mistake for the director to presume in every case that such claims come merely from one's own vivid imagination. Either of these extremes, too much gullibility in accepting everything that is claimed or a refusal to accept anything supernatural, will result in serious injury to the spiritual life of the directee. Either of these extremes will be a hindrance for the directee's relationship with God. A good spiritual director needs to know how to handle such events when the directee consults the director regarding these phenomena.

The right way for a spiritual director to handle these matters is always to be open to the possibility that this may indeed come from God. The director needs to recognize that God does frequently speak to souls in extraordinary ways and reveal himself to us in such unusual ways. We must never discount the possibility that the experience is authentically from God. One should listen very openly and take very seriously whatever is related. Then apply the test that Jesus gives us in the Sermon on the Mount: "You will know them by their fruits" (Matt 7:16).

We need to test every manifestation of the spirit, because not only can the Holy Spirit use these extraordinary spiritual phenomena to make God's Will known to us, but an evil spirit might make use of such methods to try to deceive a soul. Also, the human spirit can very easily play tricks on us. If a person wants very much to have a vision or locution from God, human imagination can very vividly provide a facsimile of a bona fide vision or locution. It is a general principle in spiritual direction that we must test every spirit. St. Ignatius writes at great length in his *Spiritual Exercises* (pp. 151–60) about the discernment of spirits. He gives many pages of explanation of how to handle this. Basically the advice of St. Ignatius is same as that of Jesus: "You will know them by their fruits."

When directees come to us with the claim that God has spoken to them or that they have had some kind of vision, first check what is said to see if it is in accord with basic Christian theology and the teachings of Christ and the Bible. If so, the directee should be advised to take quite seriously whatever has been heard or seen and then test it out. If nothing but good results, if it makes a person more humble, more loving toward God, neighbor, and self, if it helps the person to grow in faith and hope and trust in God, the probability is that the vision or locution is authentically from God.

It seems that there are some personality types and souls where God uses these extraordinary phenomena many times. Almost without exception every one of us has had at least one or two experiences of extraordinary spiritual phenomena at some time in the course of our life. Once we believe that God is real and that there is a level of life beyond this earthly life, there is every reason to believe that God does intervene in our present life on Earth. This happens not only in the ordinary ways of daily life but also God frequently intervenes in nonordinary ways in our life on Earth. For some people this happens very frequently, for most people it happens at least occasionally.

For most people these interventions of God are so gentle that often the person having them is not aware that they come from God. They are simply new ideas, new insights, new inspirations that suddenly come to us. We fail to realize that these were interventions from God in our life. This seems to be the preferred way that God acts. But if people are not open to this quiet, gentle intervention of God, then God is forced to rely on some extraordinary way to get our attention.

Often these extraordinary interventions of God in our life come at the beginning of one's conversion to God. This frequently happens when one has not taken God seriously in the early part of one's life. Then God will step into our adult life in some unusual way in order to get our attention. For others, it seems that God chooses to continue to use these extraordinary ways over and over again throughout one's life on Earth. The New Age people speak of certain persons as "channelers." Of the four gender archetypes, one is called a medium or mediatrix between the spiritual and earthly dimensions of reality. Those persons who have received an unusual share of this fourth gender archetype would seem to be the ones who have the most experiences of these extraordinary spiritual phenomena.

God is able to use one's imagination in order to reveal his Will and Word to us. This is the response that St. Joan of Arc gave to her judge when he accused her of having a very vivid imagination. St. Joan replied that of course it was her imagination, but that was the way that God used to reveal his Will to her. If the results of such interventions are good, if the person continues to grow and progress on the journey of faith, then it can be safely presumed that God is either using one's imagination or directly intervening in one's life. If the results are good, one should be encouraged to keep open to such phenomena.

Because of the danger of being led astray by an evil spirit or by one's own imagination, the directee should be urged to be open with a director regarding all such unusual phenomena. By submitting it to the objective viewpoint of the director, there is much less chance of being led astray by such events.

Modern depth psychology has clearly shown us that there is no wall of separation between the psychic world and this earthly, physical world. This is true regarding the influence our spiritual psyche has on our physical life, our bodily health and well-being. It is similarly true that there is no impenetrable wall between the transcendental, numinous level of life where God dwells and our earthly level of existence. So it is normal to expect frequent interventions from God.

It is recommended that every spiritual director read some of the masters of the spiritual life, both ancient and modern. Thus one will learn how they handled these extraordinary spiritual phenomena in their own life and in their spiritual guidance of souls who came to them for direction. Among these books would be recommended the *Spiritual Exercises* of St. Ignatius Loyola, then three books by St. Teresa of Avila, *Interior Castle, Way of Perfection,* and *Autobiography.* St. Francis de Sales has two books very helpful in discerning extraordinary spiritual phenomena. They are *Introduction to the Devout Life* and *Treatise on the Love of God*. Karl Rahner has written a book entitled *Visions and Prophecies*. Nearly a hundred years ago William James wrote *Varieties of Religious Experience,* which treats of these extraordinary phenomena from a secular point of view. Three modern books by Morton Kelsey are highly recommended for their fine treatment of unusual spiritual phenomena. They are *Encounter with God, Other Side of Silence: Meditation for the Twenty-First Century,* and *Companions of the Inner Way: The Art of Spiritual Guidance.*

Kelsey speaks of three different kinds of spiritual experience: Sacramental, Mystical, and Experiences of divine by means of images. Many spiritual directors confine their guidance to Sacramental religious experience. There is need for a director also to be familiar with the other two ways to experience God. Mystical or contemplative experiences are those experiences of the presence of God, power of God, love of God without any images. Experiences of God by means of images can be done in an active way which St. Ignatius calls "Composition of Place." One tries to project oneself back into the Gospels and imagine oneself present when Jesus works a miracle or carries out one of the Gospel events. Finally, there are the experiences of God by means of images through extraordinary spiritual phenomena such as visions or locutions.

It is not necessary for a director to have had personal mystical experiences or visions and locutions in order to be able to direct and help others who have these experiences. The less direct experience a director has of these contemplative or mystical or unusual phenomena, the more thorough should the director's knowledge be of those bona fide books that have been written by the spiritual masters of the past and present. The most important attitude the director needs to have is one of humble openness to the possibility that God has intervened in some unusual way in the life of the directee. Then listen and use one's common sense as well as intuition in trying to decide if this is indeed a help to one's faith.

Unless it is clearly evil, the normal recommendation for the spiritual director is not to make a judgment one way or the other when the directee shares an experience of unusual spiritual phenomena. Refrain from saying whether it is from God or not from God. Take a look simply at the consequences if the directee follows the message given in vision or locution. If common sense clearly indicates these consequences would not be good, then the directee should be told to ignore the message. If the consequences appear to be good, the directee should be told to take seriously the message as if it came from God. Then, later, by observing the results the director will be in a better position to decide if the vision or locution is to be trusted or not to be trusted.

For a fuller and well-balanced discussion of extraordinary mystical phenomena, the reader may consult the *New Catholic Encyclopedia,* McGraw-Hill, New York, volume 10, *Mystical Phenomena,* pages 171–74.

CHAPTER 18

Facing Death and the Cross

One of the tasks of a spiritual director is to help the directee attain to the proper Christian attitude toward death and life after death. The proper attitude is the same attitude that Jesus himself had toward his death. His human nature rebelled against the pains of his crucifixion and so he begged his Heavenly Father that, if possible, this cup of suffering might be removed from him. Nevertheless, he accepted the sufferings because it was God's Will. As far as death itself, Jesus seems to look forward to it. "Now my soul is troubled. And what should I say—'Father, save me from this hour'? No, it is for this reason that I have come to this hour. 'Father, glorify your name'" (John 12:27–28). "Then Jesus, crying with a loud voice, said, 'Father, into your hands I commend my spirit.' Having said this, he breathed his last" (Luke 23:46).

One of the more important lessons to learn on our journey of faith is the proper attitude toward death. In order to die well we need to have many dress rehearsals for death throughout our life on Earth. One way to do this is to take one day each month and try to live that day exactly the way one would want to live the last day of one's life on Earth. Such a practice will teach us detachment from the things of this world, so that when death does actually occur we can accept it in the same way that our unconscious seems to accept death. St. Paul beautifully expresses this detachment: "It is my eager expectation and hope that I will not be put to shame in any way, but that by my speaking with all boldness, Christ will be exalted now as always in my body, whether by life or by death. For to me, living is Christ and dying is gain. If I am to live in the flesh, that means fruitful labor for me; and I do not know which I prefer. I am hard pressed between the two: my desire is to depart and be with Christ, for that is far better; but to remain in the flesh is more necessary for you. Since I am convinced of this, I know that I will remain and continue with all of you for your progress and joy in faith" (Phil 1:20–25).

It is interesting that the human unconscious has this same detachment toward life and death as expressed by Jesus and St. Paul. The dreams of those who are terminally ill and know that death is imminent lack all concern about this fact of death. Death is seen by the unconscious as simply one of the facts of life and certainly not the end of life. Those who have had an after-death experience seem also to lose their fear of death. Having been given some insight into what life is like beyond physical death, they look forward to it with joy and not with dread.

By his death and resurrection Jesus reversed our normal expectations about death. Out of death comes life when that death is united to faith and trust in God. Instead of death being the end of life, for those who believe, death is merely a graduation to a higher level of life. As a result of the triumph of Jesus over death by means of his resurrection, death no longer is a thing of dread for those who believe. As the Preface of the Mass for the dead puts it, "For those who believe, life is not ended but merely changed."

The directee needs to be taught a total openness to God's Will especially in one's attitude toward death and suffering. "Anything, Lord, everything" is a wonderful way to express this detachment and openness during prayer. Since God is all-wise, all-powerful, all-good, all-loving, and always faithful to his Word and promises, we can trust God's decisions regarding life and death as always for our best interests. We need to hold on loosely to life and to all the things of earthly life. We must be willing to let go of them without looking back. "No one who puts a hand to the plough and looks back is fit for the kingdom of God" (Luke 9:62).

St. John tells us, "God is love, and those who abide in love abide in God, and God abides in them. Love has been perfected among us in this: that we may have boldness on the day of judgement, because as he is, so are we in this world. There is no fear in love, but perfect love casts out fear; for fear has to do with punishment, and whoever fears has not reached perfection in love" (1 John 4:16–18). To the extent that the directee is filled with faith, hope, and love, to that extent one is able to face death and suffering without fear.

One of the most difficult and at the same time most essential tasks of a spiritual director is to help the directee understand and accept the mystery of the cross. People need to be taught the profound meaning of the symbol of the cross in their lives. They need to be taught how to recognize and to carry the crosses that are present in their life. The situation in the world today is so critical and so serious that every Christian is called to crucifixion in one way or the other. The choices that everyone must make today will involve suffering and sacrifice. We find ourselves pulled in many different directions and not knowing which way to go. To carry the cross means that each of us has a contribution to make in resolving the evils and problems facing us today. We must allow ourselves to be stretched upon the cross of suffering. Out of this suffering and death will come new life.

The disciples were dismayed when Jesus told them not only that he would be crucified but that anyone who wished to follow him must also take up one's cross daily and follow him. The way of the cross was the path that Jesus deliberately chose to take in response to the evils of his time. What then are the crosses in our present life? The cross often comes disguised in the conflicts and contradictions in our life. Rather than running away from the difficulties that face us each day, we must like Jacob wrestle with this angel of darkness until we receive the blessing that is hidden in every cross. Some examples of crosses in our daily life are: frustration, failure, disappointment, anxiety, depression, discouragement, misunderstanding, opposition, lack of appreciation or affirmation, physical pains of all sorts, sickness, tiredness, overwork, lack of sufficient money to pay our bills, lack of love, and lack of energy. Another cross each of us is asked to carry is our lack of perfection and therefore an acceptance of our faults, cowardice, addictions, sins, and vices. Another of our crosses is to accept ownership of our negative shadow instead of projecting it on others. It is indeed a very heavy cross to have to admit to ourselves and others our envy, pride, sloth, greed, selfishness, lust, gluttony, lack of concern for others, desire for revenge, and bitterness and resentment.

When we feel depressed and lonely, do we rush out to the shopping center and buy something we don't really need, or to the ice cream parlor, or to our own refrigerator or liquor cabinet? Or do we try to carry this cross by taking a walk or visiting someone in need of our companionship? How do we act when we have to endure something contrary to what we want? Do we sulk and feel sorry for ourselves or do we bite the bullet by going ahead with the unwanted decision as peacefully as possible? When someone gives us a hard time at work or makes light of our achievements or puts us down in one way or another, do we become angry and full of revenge, saying to ourselves, "I'll get you"? Do we accept this cross by refusing to pass an evil judgment on the other person, simply saying, "I don't understand"? When we read about all the evils in the world, do we simply bemoan them or do we search for some positive response that we can make to these evils so that we try to light a candle rather than merely to curse the darkness?

All of us have to make decisions every day. Do we choose the line of least resistance or do we take up our cross and carry it as bravely as we can? Surprisingly, once we have decided to accept the crosses in our life, to wrestle with them with as much love as possible, very often we will experience a deep inner peace. This is the peace Jesus experienced when at the moment of death he said, "Father, into your hands I commend my spirit" (Luke 23:46). This inner peace results from a certain detachment from the events of this world. Once we are willing to center our life in God and in Jesus Christ, the pain is still there. Crucifixion is never painless. But amidst all the desolation and abandonment, we are able peacefully to make a total commitment into the will and hands of God. "For the message about the cross is foolishness to those who are perishing, but to us who are being saved it is the power of God....For God's foolishness is wiser than human wisdom, and God's weakness is stronger than human strength" (1 Cor 1:18, 25). God chose the way of the cross to save the world two thousand years ago and it is still the way that we must go today if we choose to do our part in saving our modern world from disaster and extinction.

Frequently we do not know the outcome of our carrying of the crosses in our life. This is especially true when we find the courage to confront the manifest evils in our society. But we can take it on faith in the words of Jesus and the New Testament writers that the way of the cross is the road to salvation. Therefore, we need to take up our cross every day in the thousand different ways that we are asked to sacrifice our will to the higher Will of God. If these crosses are carried lovingly, rejoicing with the apostles that we are judged worthy to suffer for the sake of Jesus Christ, we will surely experience a resurrection to a new and higher level of grace life. This is the paradox of the cross. With each little death to our own will and desires we will rise to a more mature wholeness and holiness.

CHAPTER 19

Facing the Future with Hope

Only God knows what the future holds. We can only guess and human predictions regarding the future have been usually mistaken in the past. Even divinely revealed prophecies regarding the future are always tentative, stating that things will go a certain way unless we repent and change our ways. The story of the prophet Jonah and his predictions regarding the destruction of Ninevah tell us exactly how we should interpret prophecies regarding the future. Also, a prophet sees the future without any depth dimension so that things that may be thousands of years apart are seen on the same level.

Today we have a choice of facing the future with positive hope or negative expectations. If we face the future in a negative way, it will destroy our enthusiasm and result in a loss of energy and zest for life. If we face the future in a positive way with hope, this will result in a great increase of energy, enthusiasm, and life. So it is very much to our advantage to face the future with hope. But do we have sufficient reason to choose hope rather than despair regarding the future? One is able to find good reasons for either the positive or negative choice. Because God usually lives up to our expectations and fulfills our hopes, it is recommended that we try to face the future with high hopes.

Father Pierre Teilhard de Chardin spent his lifetime study-ing the fossil remains of life on the planet from the past million or more years. His conclusion was that life has constantly and consistently moved forward rather than backward throughout the evolutionary course of life on this planet. There have been tragedies and setbacks when many forms of life became extinct (e.g., the dinosaurs), but there was always an attainment of a new and higher level of life at each of these critical points. As a result of his studies in paleontology, Teilhard predicted that the human race at the present time was on the verge of advancing to a new and higher level of spirituality and intelligence. Teilhard connected this historical insight of his with his intu-itions regarding Christian theology and proposed the theory of Christogenesis. He saw the human race moving forward toward what he called an *Omega point* (Omega is the last let-ter in the Greek alphabet). He called this Omega point the Cosmic Christ and saw the world moving toward the fulfill-ment of St. Paul's vision: "When all things are subjected to him, then the Son himself will also be subjected to the one who put all things in subjection under him, so that God may be all in all" (1 Cor 15:28).

Teilhard's vision of the future is somewhat similar to the vision of many of the New Age advocates who claim we are on the verge of entering a new age of the world, which they call the Age of Aquarius. The New Age people approach the future from a purely secular and astrological point of view, while Teilhard approaches it from both a scientific and Christian point of view. Teilhard disagrees with the pantheism of many of the New Age people and with their recommendation of Far Eastern philosophy's disappearance of individual personality into Nirvana. It is possible to see Teilhard's predictions regard-ing the future of the human race as similar to an individual's growth from adolescence to adulthood. It would seem that the human race as a whole has been experiencing adolescence since the Renaissance and perhaps we are now ready to move out of our teenage mentality into a more mature adulthood. According to Teilhard:

> Mankind still shows signs of a reserve, a formidable potential of concentration, that is, of progress. Think of the immensity of the powers, ideas and persons not yet discovered or harnessed or born or synthesized. In terms of energy and biology, the human race is still very young and very fresh. The earth is still far from having completed its sidereal evolution. True, we can imagine all sorts of catastrophes which might intervene to cut short this great development. But for 300 million years life has been going on paradoxically in the midst of improbability. Does this not indicate that it is marching forward, sustained by some complicity in the motive forces of the Universe? (*Building the Earth*, pp. 104–5)

There are many Christians today predicting an apocalyptic vision of the future. This is in keeping with several books of the Bible, both the Old Testament and the New Testament. The apocalyptic vision is that God has lost hope in the sinful human race and is ready to destroy it once again as in the days of Noah. This time it will be done by fire, by natural disasters such as earthquakes, and by wars and starvation. The four horsemen described in the sixth chapter of the Book of Revelation are examples of this apocalyptic vision. Similarly, the messages at Medjugorje predict dire chastisements facing the human race in the near future. The apocalyptic vision always predicts that a small number of those faithful to God will be saved but only after much suffering. One theory is that by rapture the faithful Christians will be swept up to heaven during the last days while

God is destroying the Earth, and then they will return to Earth to enjoy a thousand years of peace.

One is able to find Christians predicting and expecting the fulfillment of these apocalyptic events in almost every century of the Christian era, beginning with St. Paul and most First Century followers of Jesus. These prophets of doom were especially prominent around the year 1000 at the end of the first Christian millennium and now once again as we enter the third millennium. They were also prominent among devout Jews during the couple of hundred years previous to the birth of Jesus. Their predictions can be found in the Book of Daniel and several of the minor prophets. Until this present moment their apocalyptic predictions have not occurred. Will they be true at this present time or do we need to reinterpret these Biblical prophecies in a more positive way? We do know from the Book of Jonah that God's predictions regarding the future are always tentative and will not necessarily occur, provided we repent as did the people of Nineveh.

Alongside the apocalyptic predictions in several of the books of the Bible, we have many positive predictions regarding the future such as the one from First Corinthians on which Teilhard depended so much. The epistles to the Ephesians and Colossians also contain very positive predications regarding the future. Every spiritual director as well as every directee has to make a choice between the prophets of doom in the Bible and the prophets of hope. One can find scriptural support for either of these attitudes toward the future. Perhaps the best attitude is somewhere in the middle between these two extremes. We do need to recognize the sinfulness and evil present in our society today, both in individuals and in our institutions. We do need to repent and if we neglect to repent we can expect the natural consequences of our sins to occur. "For the wages of sin is death, but the free gift of God is eternal life in Christ Jesus our Lord" (Rom 6:23).

On the other hand, if we become prophets of doom and emphasize only the dire apocalyptic predictions regarding the future, this will dry up most of our enthusiasm for life. We lose hope and are seriously tempted to give up trying to be better. Instead, we simply wait for the axe to fall and all these terrible disasters to happen. Young people especially will be adversely affected by this negative approach to the future. I think many of the problems of youth in our present-day society are a result of this loss of hope regarding the future. In order to bring out the best in any person, one needs to have high hopes and expectations regarding the future. This is why I think the Teilhardian worldview is the one that spiritual directors should recommend to their directees. Perhaps Teilhard was too optimistic regarding the future and his optimism needs to be toned down. But his view is the way to life and to hope.

So I think we should take seriously Jesus' promise that he will never leave us orphans, that he and his Holy Spirit will always be with us. We need to take seriously the promise of God's willingness to forgive our sins regardless of how serious they might be. Basing our faith and life on these promises of God, we can hold onto hope for the future, even in the midst of any disasters, calamities, or chastisements that might happen. Let us not stick our heads in the sand and refuse to face up to the very many and manifest evils in our nation and our institutions including even our churches. The insights of the prophet Amos concerning the sins of the northern kingdom of Israel are applicable to the situation facing us today. We have bowed down in worship to the three idols of possessions, pleasure, and power. We need to repent and make better use of the three remedies of prayer, fasting, and almsgiving.

St. Thérèse of Lisieux insisted that God will live up to our expectations. If we expect a harsh judgment and condemnation by God for our sins, this is what will happen. On the other hand, if we put all our hopes and expectations in the infinite mercy, love, and goodness of God, then we can expect a very merciful judgment from God. St. Thérèse's hope was based on some very solid biblical texts, especially from second half of the Book of Isaiah and from the promises of Jesus to his disciples in the Gospels. This hope enabled Thérèse to attain a very high sanctity in the course of a very short life of twenty-four years. Several popes of this century have insisted that St. Thérèse is the best model of sanctity for our modern world. It seems to me that St. Thérèse's hope regarding God's mercy toward the sinful world not only matches but also even exceeds in some ways the optimism and hope of Teilhard de Chardin.

Rather than wringing our hands in despair and frustration, each of us is called by God to do all in his or her power to counteract the deadly spiritual virus of negativity that is present in the world today. This negativity is very contagious. If we allow it to go unchecked, countless people will become contaminated by it. Anyone who has grown up in a family environment where one or both parents were very negative can testify how hard it is to be cured of this spiritual virus. A positive, hopeful attitude toward the future is the remedy to the disease of negativity. This is the power of positive thinking about which Norman Vincent Peale tried to educate us for many years. We need to have a positive attitude of hope and expectation in five areas: toward God, ourselves, others, the world, and the future. None of these five positive attitudes will come easy in the present world situation. We will have to work hard and long at each of them before we can call them our own.

In view of the presence of so much negativity in our society today, it is recommended that a spiritual director in every session address one or more of the five positive attitudes of hope. Find biblical texts to justify each of the areas of hope. Through prayer and reflection on these scripture texts, find a number of good reasons to justify our having a positive attitude and high hopes and expectations regarding God, ourselves, others, the world, and the future. Let the director try to find in the experiences of his or her life examples of how this positive attitude of hope in each of these five areas has had good results. Encourage each directee to find similar examples of the value of optimism and hope in the directee's life or lives of people the directee might know.

The whole human race is locked today in a death-like struggle as it reluctantly lets go of the past and searches for a new way of life. We humans are a part of the whole work of creation of the new. We are called by God to be co-creators with him in bringing forth a new age, a new era of life on Earth. Each of us has a part to play, a role to fulfill. This role will be somewhat different for each of us. It is one of the main tasks of prayer to discover our particular role and then to fulfill it. "What steps must we take in relation to this forward march? I see two, which can be summarized in five words: A great hope, in common. A great hope must be born in every generous soul. Our hope will only be operative if it is expressed in greater cohesion and solidarity" (Teilhard, *Building the Earth*, pp. 107–08).

The human race today is experiencing a rite of passage from adolescence to adulthood. It is a crisis similar to what a teenager faces as one enters adult life. The human race has spent thousands of years in a childhood stage and since the Middle Ages in an adolescent stage. The present rite of passage to adulthood will probably take a century or more before it is successfully accomplished. Each of us needs to be open each day to the Holy Spirit in order to discern our unique role during these difficult times. There are at least six contributions all of us can make:

1. Have faith and trust in God to come to our rescue and help us through this crisis;
2. Create an openness to the Holy Spirit each day in prayer;
3. Develop a positive rather than negative attitude toward God, the future, the world, others, and ourselves;
4. Send out a constant stream of prayer, love, mercy, blessing, grace on the whole human race;
5. As perfectly as possible, practice the three relationships of love toward God, neighbor, and oneself;
6. Encourage, urge, teach, and help others to fulfill these six ways to assist our rite of passage.

In addition to these general ways available to all of us, we will be called to carry out other more specific tasks throughout our lifetime. Hence the importance of spending time each day in prayer in order to discern God's Will in our regard. Also, there is the need to give and receive good spiritual direction from one another since none of us are good judges in regard to our life. "Someday, after mastering the winds, the waves, the tides and gravity, we shall harness for God the energies of love. Then, for the second time in the history of the world, the human race will have discovered fire" (Teilhard, *Toward the Future*, pp. 86–87).

Bibliography

Spiritual Direction

Barry, William A. *Spiritual Direction and The Encounter with God: A Theological Inquiry.* New York/Mahwah, N.J.: Paulist Press, 1992.

————, and William Connolly. *The Practice of Spiritual Direction.* New York: Seabury Press, 1982.

Edwards, Tilden. *Spiritual Friend: Reclaiming the Gift of Spiritual Direction.* New York/Mahwah, N.J.: Paulist Press, 1980.

Fischer, Kathleen. *Women at the Well: Feminist Perspectives on Spiritual Direction.* New York/Mahwah, N.J.: Paulist Press, 1988.

Fleming, David. *Christian Ministry of Spiritual Direction.* St. Louis: Review for Religious, 1988.

Francis de Sales, St. *Introduction to the Devout Life.* Rockford, Ill.: Tan Books, 1994.

Gratton, Carolyn. *Guidelines for Spiritual Direction.* Denville, N.J.: Dimension, 1980.

Groeschel, Benedict. *Spiritual Passages: For Those Who Seek, the Psychology of Spiritual Development.* New York: Crossroad, 1990.

Jones, Alan W. *Exploring Spiritual Direction.* New York: Seabury Press, 1982.

Kelsey, Morton. *Companions on the Inner Way: The Art of Spiritual Guidance, Vol. 1.* New York: Crossroad, 1991.

———. *Encounter with God.* Minneapolis: Bethany, 1972.

Kozlewski, Joseph. *Spiritual Direction and Spiritual Directors.* Goleta, Calif.: Queenship Publishing, 1994.

Leech, Kenneth. *Soul Friend: Spiritual Direction in the Modern World.* San Francisco: Harper & Row, 1977.

May, Gerald G. *Care of Mind, Care of Spirit: A Psychiatrist Explores Spiritual Direction.* San Francisco: Harper, 1982.

Michael, Chester. *A Christian Worldview.* Charlottesville, Va.: The Open Door, 2002.

———. *A New Day.* Charlottesville, Va.: The Open Door, 2001.

Peck, M. Scott. *Further Thoughts on the Road Less Traveled.* New York: Simon & Schuster, 1993.

———. *The Road Less Traveled: A New Psychology of Love, Traditional Values and Spiritual Growth.* New York: Simon & Schuster, 1978.

Tyrell, Bernard J. *Christotherapy I.* New York: Paulist Press, 1975.

———. *Christotherapy II.* New York: Paulist Press, 1982.

Wink, Walter. *Engaging the Powers: Discernment and Resistance in a World of Domination, Vol. 3.* Minneapolis: Fortress Press, 1992.

———. *Naming the Powers: The Language of Power in the New Testament, Vol. 1.* Philadelphia: Fortress Press, 1984.

———. *Powers That Be: Theology for a New Millennium.* New York: Doubleday, 1998.

———. *Unmasking the Powers: The Invisible Forces That Determine Human Existence, Vol. 2.* Philadelphia: Fortress Press, 1986.

Yungblut, John R. *The Gentle Art of Spiritual Guidance*. New York: Continuum, 1994.

Spirituality and Prayer

Anonymous. *The Cloud of Unknowing*. Garden City, N.Y.: Doubleday, 1973.

———. *Way of the Pilgrim*. Garden City, N.Y.: Doubleday, 1978.

Chavda, Mahesh. *Prayer and Fasting*. Shippensburg, Pa.: Destiny Image, 1998.

De Caussade, Pierre. *Abandonment to Divine Providence*. New York: Doubleday, 1998.

De Mello, Anthony. *Sadhana: A Way to God, Christian Exercises in Eastern Form*. Garden City, N.Y.: Doubleday, 1984.

———. *The Song of the Bird*. New York: Doubleday, 1984.

———. *Wellsprings: A Book of Spiritual Exercises*. New York: Doubleday, 1983.

Foster, Richard J. *Challenge of the Disciplined Life: Christian Reflections on Money, Sex & Power*. New York: Harper & Row, 1985.

———. *Freedom of Simplicity: Finding Harmony in a Complex World*. San Francisco: Harper & Row, 1973.

———. *Prayer: Finding the Hearts True Home*. San Francisco: Harper, 1992.

Fox, Matthew. *Original Blessing*. New York: Penguin-Putnam, 1983.

Francis de Sales, St. *Treatise on the Love of God*. Rockford, Ill.: Tan Books, 1997.

Frankl, Viktor. *Man's Search for Meaning: An Introduction to Logotherapy*. New York: Simon & Schuster, 1984.

Fuellenbach, John. *Church: Community of the Kingdom.* Manila: Logos, 2001.

———. *Throw Fire.* Manila: Logos, 1998.

Green, Thomas H. *Drinking from a Dry Well.* Notre Dame, Ind.: Ave Maria, 1991.

———. *A Vacation with the Lord.* Notre Dame, Ind.: Ave Maria, 1984.

———. *When the Well Runs Dry: Prayer beyond the Beginnings.* Notre Dame, Ind.: Ave Maria, 1991.

Hurnard, Hannah. *Hinds' Feet on High Places.* Wheaton, Ill.: Tyndale House, 1976.

Hutchinson, Gloria. *Six Ways to Pray from Six Great Saints.* Cincinnati: St. Anthony Press, 1982.

John of the Cross, St. *Dark Night of the Soul.* New York: Doubleday, 1990.

Johnston, William. *The Inner Eye of Love.* San Francisco: Harper & Row, 1978.

———. *Letters to Contemplatives.* Maryknoll, N.Y.: Orbis, 1992.

Keating, Thomas. *Invitation to Love.* New York: Continuum, 2001.

———. *Open Mind, Open Heart.* New York: Continuum, 2000.

Kelsey, Morton. *The Other Side of Silence: Meditation for the Twenty-First Century.* New York: Paulist Press, 1976.

LaVerdiere, Eugene. *When We Pray.* Notre Dame, Ind.: Ave Maria, 1982.

Lawrence, Brother. *Practice of the Presence of God.* Staten Island, N.Y.: Alba House, 1997.

Lewis, C. S. *Mere Christianity.* San Francisco: Harper, 1952.

Maloney, George. *Prayer of the Heart.* Notre Dame, Ind.: Ave Maria, 1981.

May, Gerald G. *Addiction and Grace: Love and Spirituality in the Healing of Addictions.* San Francisco: Harper & Row, 1988.

Merton, Thomas. *Conjectures of a Guilty Bystander.* New York: Doubleday, 1965.

———. *Contemplative Prayer.* New York: Doubleday, 1972.

———. *New Seeds of Contemplation.* New York: New Directions, 1972.

Nouwen, Henri. *Beyond the Mirror: Reflections on Death and Life.* New York: Crossroad, 1980.

———. *Reaching Out: The Three Movements of the Spiritual Life.* New York: Doubleday, 1975.

———. *The Road to Daybreak: A Spiritual Journey.* New York: Doubleday, 1988.

Peck, M. Scott. *The Different Drum: Community Making and Peace.* New York: Simon & Schuster, 1987.

———. *People of the Lie: The Hope for Healing Human Evil.* New York: Simon & Schuster, 1983.

Pennington, Basil. *Centered Living: The Way of Centering Prayer.* New York: Doubleday, 1988.

Rahner, Karl. *Visions and Prophecies.* Freiburg: Herder, 1963.

Roberts, Bernadette. *The Experience of No-Self: A Contemplative Journey.* Boston: Shambhala, 1982.

———. *The Path to No-Self: Life at the Center.* Albany: State University of New York Press, 1991.

———. *What is Self?: A Study of the Spiritual Journey in Terms of Consciousness.* Austin, Tex.: Mary Botsford Goens, 1989.

Rohr, Richard, and Joseph Martos. *The Wild Man's Journey: Reflections on Male Spirituality.* Cincinnati: St. Anthony, 1996.

Rolheiser, Ronald. *The Holy Longing.* New York: Doubleday, 1999.

————. *The Shattered Lantern: Rediscovering a Felt Presence of God.* New York: Crossroad, 2001.

Sanford, John A. *The Kingdom Within: The Inner Meaning of Jesus' Sayings.* San Francisco: Harper, 1987.

Saudreau, Auguste. *The Degrees of the Spiritual Life.* New York: Benziger Bros., 1907.

Shannon, William. *Seeds of Peace.* New York: Crossroad, 1996.

Teresa of Avila, St. *Interior Castle.* New York: Doubleday, 1989.

————. *Way of Perfection.* New York: Doubleday, 1991.

Underhill, Evelyn. *Mysticism: The Nature and Development of Spiritual Consciousness.* New York: Doubleday, 1990.

Spiritual Direction and Psychology

Claremont de Castillejo, Irene. *Knowing Woman: A Feminine Psychology.* Boston: Shambhala, 1973.

Clift, Wallace. *Jung and Christianity.* New York: Crossroad, 1982.

Dourley, John. *The Illness That We Are: A Jungian Critique of Christianity, Vol. 17.* Toronto: Inner City Books, 1984.

Erikson, Erik. *The Life Cycle Completed.* New York: W.W. Norton, 1997.

Fowler, James. *Stages of Faith: The Psychology of Human Development and the Quest for Meaning.* San Francisco: Harper, 1995.

Goldbrunner, Josef. *Holiness Is Wholeness.* New York: Pantheon, 1955.

Guzie, Tad, and Noreen Guzie. *About Men and Women: How Your Great Story Shapes Your Destiny.* New York/ Mahwah, N.J.: Paulist Press, 1986.

Hall, Brian P. *The Genesis Effect: Personal and Organizational Transformations*. New York/Mahwah, N.J.: Paulist Press, 1986.

———, and Benjamin Tonna. *Hall-Tonna Inventory of Values*. New York/Mahwah, N.J.: Paulist Press, 1986.

Jung, Carl G. *Memories, Dreams, Reflections*. New York: Random House, 1989.

Keirsey, David, and Marilyn Bates. *Please Understand Me: Character and Temperament Types*. Del Mar, Calif.: Prometheus Nemesis, 1984.

Kelsey, Morton. *Christianity as Psychology: The Healing Power of the Christian Message*. Minneapolis: Augsburg, 1986.

Kohlberg, Lawrence. *The Psychology of Moral Development: The Nature and Validity of Moral Stages*. San Francisco: Harper & Row, 1984.

Kunkel, Fritz. *Creation Continues*. New York: Paulist Press, 1987.

Leonard, Linda. *The Wounded Woman: Healing the Father-Daughter Relationship*. Boston: Shambhala, 1982.

May, Gerald G. *Will and Spirit: A Contemplative Psychology*. San Francisco: Harper & Row, 1982.

Meyers, Isabel. *Gifts Differing: Understanding Personality Type*. Palo Alto, Calif.: Consulting Psychologist Press, 1980.

Michael, Chester, and Marie Norrisey. *Arise: A Christian Psychology of Love*. Charlottesville, Va.: The Open Door, 1981.

———. *Prayer and Temperament*. Charlottesville, Va.: The Open Door, 1991.

Progoff, Ira. *At a Journal Workshop: Writing to Access the Power of the Unconscious and Evoke Creative Ability*. New York: Tarchar/Putnam, 1992.

Sanford, John A. *The Invisible Partners: How the Male and Female in Each of Us Affects Our Relationships.* New York: Paulist Press, 1980.

Whitmont, Edward C. *The Symbolic Quest.* Princeton, N.J.: Princeton Univ. Press, 1991.

Life of Christ and the Bible

Borg, Marcus. *Meeting Jesus Again for the First Time: The Historical Jesus and the Heart of Contemporary Faith.* San Francisco: Harper, 1995.

Brown, Raymond. *Introduction to New Testament Christology.* New York: Paulist Press, 1994.

Goodier, Alban. *Public Life of Our Lord Jesus Christ (Volumes I & II).* Boston: St. Paul, 1990.

Guardini, Romano. *The Lord.* Washington, D.C.: Regnery Gateway, 1982.

Michael, Chester. *The Human Side of Jesus.* Charlottesville, Va.: The Open Door, 2001.

Morton, H. V. V. *In the Steps of the Master.* New York: Dodd Mead, 1962.

Lives of the Saints

Augustine, St. *Confessions of St. Augustine.* New York: Doubleday, 1960.

Day, Dorothy. *The Long Loneliness: The Autobiography of Dorothy Day.* San Francisco: Harper & Row, 1981.

Furlong, Monica. *Thérèse of Lisieux.* London: Virago, 1987.

Goerres, Ida. *The Hidden Face.* New York: Pantheon, 1959.

Thérèse of Lisieux, St.. *Autobiography of Saint Thérèse of Lisieux: The Story of a Soul.* New York: Doubleday Image, 1957.

Welch, John. *Spiritual Pilgrims.* New York: Paulist Press, 1982.

Miscellaneous

Berne, Patricia and Louis Savary. *Dreams and Spiritual Growth*. New York/Mahwah, Paulist Press, 1984.
———. *Dream Symbol Work*. New York/Mahwah, Paulist Press, 1991.

Berry, Thomas. *The Dream of the Earth*. San Francisco: Sierra Club, 1988.

Brewi, Janice, and Anne Brennan. *Mid-Life*. New York: Crossroad, 1991.

Coleman, Bill, and Patty Coleman. *Whispers of Revelation: Discovering the Spirit of the Poor*. Mystic, Conn.: Twenty-Third Publications, 1992.

Covey, Stephen. *The 7 Habits of Highly Effective People: Powerful Lessons in Personal Change*. New York: Simon & Schuster, 1989.

Douglass, James W. *Nonviolent Coming of God*. Maryknoll, N.Y.: Orbis, 1993.

Dwyer, John. *Church History*. New York: Paulist Press, 1991.

Eisler, Riane. *The Chalice and the Blade: Our History, Our Future*. San Francisco: HarperSan Francisco, 1988.

Haring, Bernard. *My Hope for the Church*. Liguori, Mo.: Liguori, 1999.

James, William. *Varieties of Religious Experience,* New York. Longmans, Green, 1925.

Kübler-Ross, Elisabeth. Death, *The Final Stage of Growth,* Englewood, Prentice-Hall, 1975.

Moody, Raymond. *Life after Life, Atlanta,* Mockingbird Press, 1975.

Puhl, Louis. *The Spiritual Exercises of St. Ignatius*. Chicago, Loyola University Press, 1951.

Teilhard de Chardin, Pierre. *Building the Earth*. Denville, N.J., Dimension, 1965.

————. *Christianity and Evolution.* New York, Harcourt Brace, 1969.

————. *The Divine Milieu.* New York, Harper & Brothers, 1960.

————. *Toward the Future.* New York, Harcourt Brace, 1975.